Unsilenced:
The Spirit of Women

Unsilenced:
The Spirit of Women

Edited and Compiled by
Mollie Cox Bryan

With a Foreword by
Lynn Andrews, author of "The Medicine Woman Series"

Commune-A-Key Publishing
Salt Lake City, Utah

Commune-a-Key Publishing
P.O. Box 58637
Salt Lake City, UT 84158
(801) 581-9191
(801) 581-9196 Fax

Library of Congress Cataloging-in-Publication Data
Unsilenced: the spirit of women / edited and compiled by Mollie Cox
Bryan: with a foreword by Lynn Andrews.
    p. cm.
    Includes index.
    ISBN: 1-881394-11-5 (ppk.: alk. paper)
    1. American literature—Women authors. 2. Women—United
States—Literary collections. 3. American literature—20th century.
4. Women—United States. I. Bryan, Mollie Cox, 1963-   .
PS508.W7U57 1997
810.8'09287'0904—dc21   97-3126
                                          CIP

$14.95 U.S. – Prices may vary outside of the U.S.

Editorial: Caryn Summers
Cover Design: Lightbourne Images, Ashland, OR
Photo credits: Shannon Caudill, Copyright © 1997.

Permission to reprint the following poems was granted by:

"Pagan" from HER BLUE BODY EVERYTHING WE KNOW,
EARTHLING POEMS. Copyright © 1991 by Alice Walker. Reprinted by
permission of Harcourt Brace & Company.

"The Breathing, The Endless News," and "Dialectical Romance," from
GRACE NOTES by Rita Dove. Copyright © 1989 by Rita Dove. Reprinted
by permission of the author and W.W. Norton & Company, Inc.

"Lord, in My Heart" from OH, PRAY MY WINGS ARE GONNA FIT ME
WELL by Maya Angelou. Copyright © 1975 by Maya Angelou.
Reprinted by permission of Random House, Inc.

"The Great Charge" and "Initiation of the Shaman Drums" from THE
HOLY BOOK OF WOMEN'S MYSTERIES, by Z. Budapest. Copyright ©
by Z. Budapest. Reprinted by permission of the author.

Dedicated with admiration to Tillie Olsen:
and
with love to the women who made me what I am (whatever that is) –
Mom, Grandma, Greatgrandma, Aunt Marty, and Aunt Judy;
and
with neverending gratitude to the Queen of Heaven.

*Special thanks to Caryn Summers for her passionate belief in this book
and to her colleagues at Commune-a-Key for all their hard work.*

And to the contributors...may you forever be unsilenced.

Table of Contents

The Feminine

The Family

The Loss

The Self

Spirituality

Foreword

— by Lynn Andrews —

My search for a teacher began thirty years ago, when as a younger woman I was looking for an understanding of the special gifts I have been given in my life. I have always been able to see lights around people and dark places in their bodies which represent energy knots or disease. I did not understand these gifts until I met my teachers, Agnes Whistling Elk and Ruby Plenty Chiefs. These two women teachers helped me to find my "voice" in life. Having a voice means that you have moved through the energy knots that society leaves you with— your conditioning as a child, sources of fear, places of unreality, as well as areas within your body not fully communicated, and places of disharmony that will eventually create disease if you don't deal with the stresses and tensions that cause them.

Finding a voice means knowing the personal way you relate to your God. When you relate to your God, your heart opens, and you are filled with gratefulness for your existence, gratefulness for the magic of your body, gratefulness for the life force that animates you and all living things. How can you look around at the simplest form in nature and not feel grateful? When you experience gratefulness, your heart opens, and a connection with God, the Great Spirit, is created. In that connection is a sense of prayer, a sense of light, a sense of silence and listening: a deep listening to the life that flows around you, a sincere listening for the words of Creation that define your voice. You don't need to tell Creation what you are doing. The All-knowing knows what you're going to say and supports your voice as you express your reality.

While I was writing *Walk in Spirit, Prayers for the Seasons of Life,* a collection of prayers accentuating the sacredness of the Earth's seasons, I realized that prayer is not a "wordful" thing. The essence of woman, too, is not a "wordful" thing. The essence of woman is the womb, the sacred void that all women carry. It is in the silence that you find your voice. Your power dwells in silence—that place of stillness at the center of the storm where you stand, unaffected, yet totally affected by the consciousness and force of life around you. Finding your voice is finding your silence; a chosen and deliberate quietude, not an imposed one.

As I read *Unsilenced: The Spirit of Women,* a book compiled by powerful and courageous women, I came to a place of stillness within myself, a place of listening, a place of wanting to hear and feel and understand not only the words, but the hearts of these women. Each story or poem reveals a different aspect of a woman's voice, as well as her silence. When you consider the beauty of what woman is, that sacred void, you see that she carries the receptiveness of Creation and creativity within. That is a prayer in itself. These women have found a voice to express that prayer through their words and their acts of creative power.

Through these women you understand that an act of power is a great teacher. When you make a true act of power and create something that is a statement made through your words, it comes from that place of passion in your heart and soul. When you look in the mirror, that act of power creates you, and you see who you are—the good aspects of yourself and the hidden places that feel incomplete. The places that are incomplete or inadequate, are perhaps, your greatest teachers. Here is where you begin to learn what your voice truly yearns to express. An act of power is an experience, not just of words, but also your silence.

When I say that communication with God—the Great Spirit, the Goddess Mother—is within moments of silence, I mean that those are moments for us to relate to one another, to grow, and to help one another. We need to communicate those precious times when we're alone with ourselves and our demons. Those moments can help others. We know that we are not actually alone, that we walk this path with our sisters, helping one another to grow and create. We can teach each other as women by sharing our circle of truth.

We do this by not holding our power in our throats, strangling from the silenced words, afraid to speak unless spoken to, afraid to be heard. We do this by speaking from the heart. Love and the connection with the Great Spirit is created when you speak from your heart as the women in this wonderful book have.

This is an inspiring and beautiful collection of intimate moments and intimate communication. When you speak the language of the spirit, your wisdom becomes an offering of your being, and your life becomes a prayer and an art form. Reading this book will truly help you find your voice and speak from your heart. I know these stories will unsilence your power and bring you closer to your Creator.

Lynn V. Andrews, author of
The Medicine Woman Series and
Love & Power, a Fall 1997 release from Harper Collins, N.Y.

Preface

"These are not natural silences, that necessary time for renewal, lying fallow, gestation, in the natural cycle of creation. The silences I speak of here are unnatural; the unnatural thwarting of what struggles to come into being, but cannot. In the old, the obvious parallels; when seed strikes stone; the time is drought or blight or infestation; the frost comes premature....

How much it takes to become a writer. Bent (far more common than we assume), circumstances, time, development of the craft—but beyond that: how much conviction as to the importance of what one has to say, one's right to say it. And the will, the measureless store of belief in oneself to be able to come to, cleave to, find the form for one's own life comprehensions. Difficult for any male not born into a class that breeds such confidence. Almost impossible for a girl, a woman."

– Tillie Olsen, *Silences*

Oh, how these words have touched me. How I continually go back to my old, worn, torn, and tattered copy of *Silences*. I go to it for strength, resolve, and empowerment. Tillie Olsen's words resonated within me from the moment that I read them. These words often give me the energy and fortitude I need to finish that last revision on a poem or essay or to write one more query letter.

This anthology presents a group of women—including me—who have found the time in our hectic schedules of varying "busyness" to etch out a piece for ourselves, our art, and our spirit. We may use our lunchtimes at the office, we may arise at 5:00 a.m., or we may wait until our babies are fully grown and out the door, but we are slowly, meticulously etching the time for ourselves. Filling our silences.

And these silences are everywhere in women's lives—not just in their art and creativity. I feel that when it exists in something as basic as our spirituality—as it does for millions of women who are frustrated in the mainstream faiths that are male dominated—it will permeate every facet of our lives. When women find their voices, they also find their art and spirit (or lack of it). This time and space is a magical, healing place in women's lives.

"When women find their voices, they also find their art and spirit (or lack of it)."

With this in mind, I collected writing from contemporary women of all faiths, ages, and levels of writing. This collection provides a wide spectrum of views and talents.

Included in it are women like Stephanie Noble, who has written one book and is a prolific and consistent writer, and women like Sheila Gorg, who after years of raising children and involvement in the church and community is just finding her voice as a writer. Among the many voices you will read and rejoice with are some of our foremost women writers including Maya Angelou, Z. Budapest, Alice Walker, Rita Dove and Lynn Andrews.

Please do not read this book with an academic eye. If you do, you may be pleased but you will be missing out on the spirit of the collection. All of the women who have contributed to these pages are celebrating the unsilenced expression of their heart and souls—let it rise to your emotions and fill your senses.

Collecting material for this book has been a tremendously enriching experience for me. I chose writing that elicited a gut reaction from me, not writing that is artistically brilliant (although in many cases, it truly is). I have become a part of this diverse community of women writers who have a common ground—they have something to say. Listen.

– *Mollie Cox Bryan*

The Creation

"Interconnection is the understanding that all being is inter-related, that we are linked with all of the cosmos as parts of one living organism. What affects one of us affects us all."

– Starhawk, *The Spiral Dance*

Women have always had a strong, undeniable link to the cycles of the earth and the pull of the moon. When we allow ourselves, we can feel this interconnection.

The women who write in this section are singing the praises of nature, healing through it, and often, worshipping it.

We are born to live awhile, to die, to return
Our physical matter to the pool of universal stuff
from which everything is made and remade,
To rejoin our spiritual force with the
unseen fields of energy that grid the universe.

from *As one of countless creations*
by Jean Carpenter

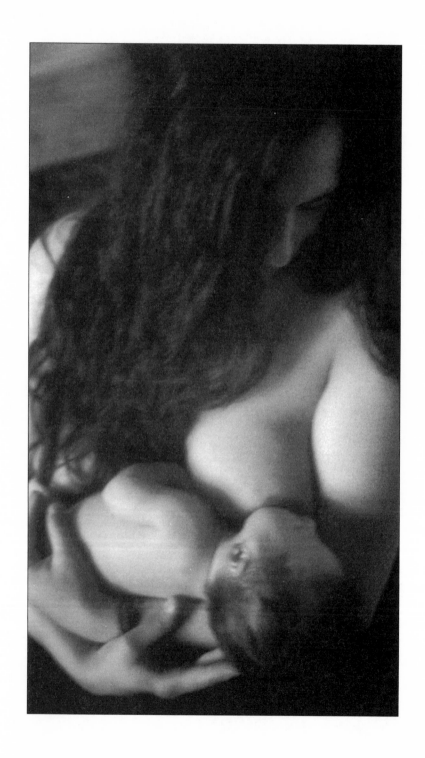

Woman's Work

The contractions come
the first waves of a rising tide
lapping at the shore
of this island
I have become
I retreat to the center
ready for woman's work

I am not alone
He who shared in conception
Takes my hand in his

I am not alone
These sensations,
growing ever stronger and more
    demanding,
sing of my connection to every woman
every female mammal, baaing,
    mooing and meowing
as she brings forth new life

Opening, a bud flowering
a universe unfolding
Galaxies whirl, while I
at the vortex
am consumed in the denseness
of life's sweetest mystery
generation upon generation
thrusting forth through me

Thousands of years of western
    civilization are shed
as I rise and fall with these sensations
I cry, I yell, I sweat, I curse,
I am woman unleashed, untamed
I am all things wet and dark and rich
I am the soil that burgeons forth
    new life
I am spring itself

Sensations pound at floodtide
Hurricane, tornado, earthquake, volcano
Nature unleashed in the micro-
    climate of my body
And then, just when it seems that
    this storm will last forever
—Just when I have forgotten why I
    am here
and what is being promised—
dawn comes and
he who has been a hiccup,
a kick, a movement,
now has voice
I hear his mewling cry
and tears of joy run down my cheeks
He is in my arms, small and fragile
    and pink
Moist and crumpled, wrinkled and sage
I look into his face
and fall in love.
In the wake of the storm
new life begins.

– *Stephanie Noble*

Mitakuye-Oyasin

Earth Mother
Loves her Children.
We are all related.

From the Finned
To the Feathered,
From the Legged
To the Rooted,
Creepers and Crawlers.

We are all Her children.
We are all related.

The Weak and the Strong.
The Rich and the Poor.
The Young and the Old.
Swift and Slow.

We are all Her children.
We are all related.

With Love and Hate, Joy and Pain,
Life and Death,
We are related.

Yesterday, Today, and Tomorrow,
Here and There,
You and Me,
We are all Related.
We are all Her children.

– Gina Jones

Caribbean Altar

Turquoise water ripples
and foams
around my sandy feet—
                                  cleansing.
Fine, white, sun-heated sand
    blankets
earth; palm trees dance, swaying
    in sky.
Roaring hushes rise from
    ocean.
Rhythmic pulses blend with
    bongo.
Giant sea rocks look like
    ancient
cathedrals. Crystal clear
    water
embraces me with warmth.
    Rainbow
colored fish scatter from
    my view.
I kiss a salty sea shell
    seeking
the healing hand of a
    sacred
Sea Goddess for strength,
    resolve,
and guidance. I kneel at Her
    altar,
Sea bird cries to blue sky,
    echoes
in tropical wind. I cry
    to ghosts
of lust, love, and passions
    Divorced.
Yet now, I Feel moon-pulled
    waves.

Caribbean breeze cools
hot flesh.
Rains come hard and quickly
                            move on.

– Mollie Cox Bryan

Healing

She walked along the wooded path
   with trees
     casting shadowed patterns
    as the sun shone
  through their leaves.
Inhaling the freshness
  of life
    renewing her spirit
      through the scents
  she felt the heaviness
    of her life.....evaporate.
Coming upon a tree stump
    freshly cut
  she stepped upon it
  gently, lightly, softly
  not wishing to cause it
    further pain.
Tall and straight she stood
  in human form
    looking, reaching, seeking
   the sun,
   the blueness above
   and more.
Eyes closed, breathing deeply
  her body swayed
   rhythmically, gracefully
    tree-like entrancement
   one with nature
   and its life force.
She becomes one with the tree,
  with life
  its energy and spirit
   fill her soul
 wholly....holy
   she is free at last.

– *Virginia Butchart Cowie*

6

Solstice

Comes midwinter
The mystery draws near
The darkness closes in
The cold deepens.
Against the chill turn you inward
Touch those gone before
Listen for the ancient litanies
The assurance of death and renewal.
Pass the light on to the new year
To the generation that comes after.

Touch the mystery and live.

– Jean Carpenter

What is joy
but an exultation of larks, ascending,
rising, chests to the sky,
hearts brimming, beating,
at the universe's perfection?

– *Susan Galbraith*

Praise and Wonder

Praise for the evergreens, silently holding their peace at every hour;
   the pine cone rosettes, scattered hopefully across the crusted snow;
   the winter's cornfield, its pale stubble inviting me,
   inviting the flock of hungry geese;
Wonder at the thick gray trail of sticks left in the meadow
   by last year's river belly;
   the upturned tree, exposing its own roots and
   claiming strength in any position;
   the brown leftover leaves, reshuffling with each wind,
   mating in the rain and in the snow;
Praise for the gray stone wall that knows its place and marks
   the passing of each day's light;
   the tufted beards of grass covering the hillside;
   the edge of ice fastened to the river and licked into a curve
   by the sun and the moving black water.
Wonder at the smooth rocks surfacing in the meadow,
   each rounded and waiting like somebody's mother;
   the jagged rock ledges, jutting through the earth
   to heal wounds in the sun;
   the nourishing secret berries of the woods,
   shriveling undiscovered.
Sing at the red marsh grasses, sprouting from ice,
   feeding the hungry gray eye;
   the final traces of the season's snow, melting
   into mystical patterns at the edge of my shoe;
I am for this life, full of little deaths and little lives
   touching each of us, like so many raindrops
   cupped in our fingers;
I am for all the lives that came before, singing, digging,
   shaping vessels of the the earth and planting fruit trees,
   not only for their fruits but for their blossoms;
I am for all the lives that will come after, bowing to the winds of spring;
   touching the soil with their hands, and
   tasting praises with their lips.

– Connie Hershey

As one of countless creations

As one of countless creations
that constitute one planet,
Itself an organism among many others
making up a universe that may be
yet another organism in yet another entity,

We are born to live awhile, to die, to return
Our physical matter to the pool of universal stuff
from which everything is made and remade,
To rejoin our spiritual force with the
unseen fields of energy that grid the universe.

Our immortality rests not in some nebulous heaven,
Nor in historical fame, nor even in human memory.
Whether or not we "go gently into the good night,"
Go we surely will, and just as surely come
back again, redistributed in other forms and souls.

–Jean Carpenter

To Valhalla

Everything fits into this life

This life that is a resolute, moving
boat, alone in a fog
that rests
on a curve of prow
in shape of black sail;
slow current turning keel to
a westward tide.

This life that is a silent Viking craft,
touched by the dying sun
not burning yet, not tinder,
flowered bier still,
    Imbedded in an unconscious sea
this hollow vessel
face the direction
of the moon (where the moon will be)...

Take what is needed for that afterlife,
that is, nothing;
everything fits here,
and
is useless beyond.

– Laura H. Kennedy

Spiritual Influences

1

Immerse yourself in me:
the stuff you were conceived of,
that cushioned you
before you were born,
that John the Baptist
sprinkled upon bent heads,
that you now imbibe and excrete.

You are water too.
You flow.
You freeze.
You build a dam.
You thaw.
You are blocked by ice.
Ice jams beget floods.

2

God created the flood
before the rainbow.
If I were not water
I would choose to be a dove,
circling above
my own reflection
looking for peace.
If I found an olive branch,
I would offer it for shelter
within your cupped hands.

3
My sins wash away
through storm sewers
that symbolize
the blocked bowel
of suburbia.

But when I walk in the rain
I remember
God is infinite water.

Even the rainbow
reminds me
of all your broken promises,
pear-shaped units of water,
the indefinite mist
we aspire to become.

– Joanne Seltzer

In Celebration of the Winter Solstice

Do not be afraid of the darkness.
Dark is the rich fertile earth that cradles the seed, nourishing
growth. Dark is the soft night that cradles us to rest.
Only in darkness can stars shine across the vastness of space.
Only in darkness is the moon's dance so clear.
There is mystery in the darkness, born in the quiet hours.
There is magic in the darkness

Do not be afraid,
We are born of this magic.
It fills our dreams that root and unravel and reweave
themselves only in the shelter of darkness.
Darkness has its own hue, its own resonance, its own breath.
It fills our soul
Not with despair, but with promise
Darkness is the gestation of our deep and knowing self
Darkness is the cave in which we rest and renew our soul
We are born of the darkness, and each night we return
to the dark moist womb of our beginnings

Do not be afraid of the darkness
for the darkness lets our own inner light shine brighter
Our guiding light
The light of love and knowing
As we fan the flame of our inner light, the darkness recedes
As we shed our light we also shed our fear of the darkness
All is revealed

Do not rush the coming of the sun.
Do not crave the lengthening of the day.
Celebrate the darkness.
Here and now. A time of richness. A time of joy.

Happy Solstice.

– Stephanie Noble

Anthem

In the deep and quiet wood
You can hear it:
A softly whispered sound,
An ancient sound
Warm as a womb and growing deeper
With each turning of the earth.

The trees hear it and recognize,
Their branches shudder with
A steady, mounting joy.
The mountains hear it—
Like mammoth breasts they sit
In their protecting circle, and wait.

The sound becomes,
Rolls into a dawning sound,
A sounding song long awaited:
All our ancient mothers' voices
Rising slowly from the
Deep and quiet wood,
Rising in glory

Rising in reclamation.

– Mary Diane Hausman

To Butterfly Woman

She followed Moonlight
To find her path.
She listened to Music-makers
To hear her heart.

But she could not hear.
She could not see.

She walked the stretch of sand
To see where she had come.
She climbed mountain changes
To change herself.

But she could not remember.
She could not change.

She followed bee's circles
To join their understanding.
She dove into cold waters
To awaken her breath.

But it was too cold, too fast.
She could not join.

Then walking amidst the darkness
She saw her shadow.
Following her,
Mirroring her,
Blinding her.

So she stopped.
Reflecting in.
Looking out.
She simply sat.

On wings they came
Discovering her.
Joining her.
Circling her.

Butterflies fluttered about her.

Changing her.
Remembering her.
Seeing her.
Hearing her.

Resting.
They rested with her.
Opening.
They opened to her.

– Gina Jones

Thou Shalt Protect Thy Habitat

She sat alone on the high ridge where she could watch the sunset. She was always alone now. It had been many months, maybe a year or more, since she had seen another living creature. The nonliving ones—that was different. The spirits that crowded her dreams, both sleeping and waking, had become a restless horde. They so crowded her awareness that sometimes she felt she was suffocating, but of late they were all the company she had, and she welcomed them.

In the beginning, she had scrupulously kept track of the passing months and years. It had seemed important then; maybe someone, sometime, would want to know how it had happened, and how much time had passed. But now she knew it was futile. The inexorable certainty had crept into her very bones and gradually from there into her dreams and eventually into her consciousness, that none of her kind would come this way again.

> *"Then the planet had been a living thing, host to an interwoven system of endlessly diverse creatures and plant life."*

Sometimes she wondered idly whether there might, somewhere, be others like her—others who had managed to find enough food in the ever-dwindling fields, forests, and streams to eke out meager survival. But she could no longer bring herself to care very deeply. Even if there were others, they, too, would be running out of companions, out of food, and out of the will to live. She hated to admit it—she had never been a quitter—but it was all too evident that their time was finished.

It was when she looked back to the old days that she wanted to grieve—to the time before the climate went haywire, before spreading hunger and desperation spawned multiple wars for land and water, before the have-nots wiped out the haves (and eventually themselves as well) with small-scale nuclear encounters and bacteriological invasions. Then the planet had been a living thing, host to an interwoven system of endlessly diverse creatures and plant life. They had had so much, but they had destroyed it and thrown it all away, and she wept quietly for the dying earth.

She had grown accustomed to silence and lifeless brown vistas, but she could still find beauty, and she stayed until the sun's golden splendor was no longer visible. Thinking wearily of the walk back to her shelter, she pulled herself slowly and carefully erect. The rocks displaced by her feet rolled away with a dry rattling sound, and for a few moments, that was all she heard. But as the rattle died away, she became aware of another sound—a rustle that started, and stopped, and started again. She bent over again, her weakened muscles trembling, to bring her eyes and ears closer to the ground, and finally she spotted it. A small black bug—a beetle of some sort she thought—was scrabbling around in the dust as if he thought there was a reason for living. She continued watching in bemused pity for his delusion, until he found his hole and disappeared from view.

It was then that she saw the patch of green—just a few thin blades of some grassy weed—and she stared as though she had never seen such a thing before. She found herself on her knees, cupping her hands around the precious growth, all her instincts to shelter and nurture rising like a warm tide that spilled over in tears again. "Too late," she whispered. "Too late."

She was enthralled, a little, by the unaccustomed sound of her own words, so she spoke again, soothingly, like a mother to a child. "I know, I know, it's too late for us. But you can make it—yes, you can." She lay on the ground, curling her body protectively around the fragile patch of green. The night chill began to seep into her bones, and her muscles were too weak even to shiver, but she couldn't leave. Grief still clung to her soul, but now there was a tiny green thread of hope. It wasn't the earth that was fragile, only the habitat. Her kind had been a mistake, an evolutionary error that the earth had purged from its system, but the planet was strong, and its recovery had already begun. She huddled there, offering her last warmth to the new life she had found.

–*Jean Carpenter*

Fragile

God,
    It's amazing
    that You love us—
        Understanding us
        as You do.

But then I see
    dust
    rising on the wind
    and understand
    You understand
        our fragility,
        knowing from
        what it is
        that we are made.

– Nancy Spiegelberg

myth

he made us
from intense ingredients
liquids that bubbled
in those first mad moments
a man and a woman
coming from that crazy cry
that unbearable storm
that glued us
sex to sex
he linked us out
from the stuff of private tears
and nights without notions
or wind
or hearts
or poets screaming at the world
that is how we came
from one tense time
before god was father
and still stood firm as stone
a youth who sang about his creation!

and this is the system
we have all figured out
that dust equals religion
our hearts come from the reddest flames
we like to say
and our heads pulled out with
long black tongs
from his deep green soul
his deep green soul!

— Su Byron

Healing the Wound

"When we speak about the specific value poetry has for responding to pain and trauma, it is important to remember there was a time when it was natural for people to consider poem-making and the creative imagination essential for both healing and guidance. The Greek wisdom culture, the enlightened society of the Vedas, and Native American peoples—all used language, and the creative imagination to communicate healing and serve as a guide for living."

–John Fox, *Finding What You Didn't Lose*

Every wound is sacred—from very personal, emotional traumas to physical illness and injury. We reach out through poem and story to heal our wounds.

The writers in this section have taken great personal risk in putting pen to paper, opening up their wounds, revealing themselves to you, and more importantly, to themselves. You will read of many wounds and many modes of healing on the pages that follow. Some women write of healing from breast cancer, some from sexual abuse, and some from spiritual emptiness. Whatever their wound, these women are all on a journey of healing.

> *She has been burned,*
> *blackened by the ashes of time,*
> *Singed by sexual sickness,*
> *Burned by betrayal.*
> *I see her and know she is me.*

from *Face in the Fire*
by Virginia Butchart Cowie

Face in the Fire

She was golden with blackened cheeks.
Her eyes were slits, unseeing or closed.
How radiant she appeared,
Through a sadness.
She was the face I saw in the fire.

She has been burned,
blackened by the ashes of time,
Singed by sexual sickness,
Burned by betrayal.
I see her and know she is me.

I have been through the hellfires of life.
And I am still here.
I've grown strong and bold.
The victim crumbles,
And leaves a golden goddess of strength.

Through tarnish and scars I am beautiful.
My strength comes from within,
My beauty, from the soul.
From life's firing,
I have emerged from the kiln...whole.

– *Virginia Butchart Cowie*

the lord said to me through clenched teeth

the lord said to me through clenched teeth
stop sobbing
the light kept flickering on and off
I thought I would start falling
stop gushing with feeling
he sent this old angel
old woman with black boots
who smelled from whiskey and bread
enjoy life
she said
put your heart behind you
her black teeth rotted as she spoke
and fell from old lips
enjoy your life!
her voice crashed from beyond her
what color were her eyes?
O I cannot I cannot
tell you

– Su Byron

Daddy

do I still love him?
did I ever?
Was it love
or clinging strings of
dependence
reinforced
with guilt?
Twisted ties
bound and gagged
by duty
and appearances.
By the rules that decree
families love each other.
Always.
Blood is thicker
than water.
But water, clean and pure,
as ties of blood were not.
Things instead of time.
Lies instead of truth.
Betrayal of the trust
that he was father
i was child.
A bond sacred and unsullied,
shattered and soiled.
its broken pieces
lodged in heart and soul
only now working their
razor-like way
to light.
Buried beneath illusions
beneath a dollhouse
beneath polished stones
and gleaming metal.

Markers that could not keep the
ghosts from rising.
A burial mound that could not
prevent
the Resurrection.
Did I love him? Perhaps.
Do I love him? No, I don't.
But loving him
and not loving him
really don't feel
all that different.

– Kathryn Elizabeth Antea

Two Grandmothers

Groping my way back to consciousness through the anesthesia fog, I focused hard on the benign face of my surgeon, looking for a sign of reassurance. I found none. Evenly, without emotion, he formed the words. "We found a little cancer in there."

The room turned icy, my heart stumbled, and my visceral cry of anguish became entrapped in my throat. So this is what it feels like to be dealt your death sentence at forty-five, I thought. My brain wailed its silent response, "My God! I am going to die!" But the words that came out of my mouth were, instead, "Can we save my breast?"

"Let's worry about saving your life first," was Dr. P.'s calm, kindly measured reply.

Life after a cancer diagnosis was a concept that lacked reality for me. Breast cancer had stolen away my beloved grandmother, my father's mother, in her early fifties, leaving me—her only granddaughter—a broken-hearted twelve-year-old who had lost not only her grandmother but also her confidant, her soulmate, her very best friend.

We had been so much alike: introspective, nongregarious, uncomfortably shy—with a propensity for holding hurts inside. Grandma Gertie's intensely private personality probably cost her life. I later learned that she had discovered her own breast lump but had told no one except her husband, who honored her wishes not to divulge her secret to physician or family. In those days—in a small Iowa town in the early 1950s—some things simply "weren't talked about." Breast cancer was one of them. And so Grandma's cancer spread to her other breast. And ultimately to her brain. And even though she eventually sought medical treatment and endured first one, then a second, radical mastectomy, her life could not be saved. She died at home, as she wished, propped up in a bed moved onto the enclosed porch at the front of my grandparents' home so that she could see the tree limbs through the windows.

My husband, Bruce, recalls my first words to him in the recovery room after my biopsy: "I'm really pissed!"

The raw, naked, ineloquently expressed truth was out. And it was true. I was angry. Angry because I had embraced a healthful lifestyle several years earlier—given up smoking, taken up regular exercise, trimmed off an excess fifteen pounds—and looked and felt the picture of health. Angry because my trim, physically fit body had turned against me. Angry because I had so much more living to do. Our younger daughter was still in high school and very much still in need of a mother; our two grandchildren, ages four and two, would be too young to remember me if I died now. Bruce and I were just beginning to sample and nurture the twoness of our relationship and the pleasures of empty-nester years, travelling to places long dreamed about.

A catalytic mixture of my anger and Bruce's constant love and support fueled a dizzying whirl wind of activity during the succeeding weeks as we sought medical opinions from oncologists, radiologists, surgeons, and plastic surgeons; talked with experts at the National Cancer Institute and the American Cancer Society; and read mountains of literature about breast cancer and its treatments. The number of options was both heartening and disturbing. After listening to all the medical advice and sifting through all the printed matter, the decision about my course of treatment was ultimately ours alone to make. It was a weighty responsibility.

Our research took us to Georgetown University's Radiology Department, where an empathetic doctor examined me, studied my biopsy and mammogram results, and unhurriedly answered our myriad questions. No, I was not, in his opinion, a candidate for lumpectomy-followed-by-radiation treatment. For one thing, my mammogram showed a second area of calcification in the same breast as the original cancer site: the cancer had spread. Therefore my breast would have to be irradiated in two places, leaving burned tissue in the section where the radiation beams would cross. The radiologist was sure that the cosmetic results would be unsatisfactory. In addition, he was not nearly so confident, as Dr. P. had been, that I would prove not to have lymph-node involvement, a determination that would require a node dissection in the course of further treatment.

One of the most discouraging experiences in our opinion search was our consultation with the Oncology Department at Johns Hopkins University Medical Center. The oncologists there gave the bleakest prognosis we had heard in our information quest—a far lesser survivability rate based on my having two cancer sites in one breast. The Johns Hopkins doctors proposed a modified-radical mastectomy followed by a CAF chemotherapy regimen, a more rigorous and far more debilitating course of treatment than the typical CMF treatment usually prescribed for breast-cancer patients.

Considerably dispirited, we sought the opinions of two more oncologists. One, Dr. S. of Bethesda, Maryland, had been recommended by an American Cancer Institute employee. Even though I ultimately selected an oncologist closer to home and within my company's HMO plan, I owe a debt of gratitude to Dr. S. for the insightful words that Bruce and I pinned our hopes on from that day forward: "At one year (of survival), pour a glass of champagne. At three years make it a bottle of champagne. At five years, buy a case of Dom Perignon and invite all your friends!" On that day, Dr. S. lit the candle of hope for us — yes, people do live for one, three, even five years and beyond after breast cancer!

Even though the evidence was mounting in favor of a mastectomy and adjuvant chemotherapy, we made one last-ditch effort to locate a radiologist willing to tackle my case without necessitating further surgery. Through our contact at Georgetown University, we learned of a prominent New York radiologist, Dr. H., who had been experimenting with innovative techniques in cancer treatment. We rushed my medical records to New York City for his scrutiny and consulted with him by telephone. He expressed willingness to try radiation therapy, should I elect that course of treatment, but echoed the earlier prediction of an unattractive cosmetic result.

And so the die had been cast for a modified-radical mastectomy. I had read several accounts by women who had undergone mastectomies, and some of their remembrances of coming out of anesthesia to witness the horror of a missing breast were vivid in my memory, as were their reports of impaired sexual responsiveness. Bruce continually reassured me that he loved me, not my breasts, and that he would steadfastly support whatever decision I made. I was not confident that my own emotional state was sufficiently strong to deal with a delayed breast reconstruction, and so—once the decision for mastectomy had been made—the decision for an immediate reconstruction was nearly simultaneous.

Selecting this course of treatment led to yet another decision to be made: whether an abdominal flap or a silicone implant. The plastic surgeon I selected, Dr. S. at Georgetown University Medical Center, favored the flap as being closest to the natural breast in feel and appearance. However, it would require a longer convalescence, and my sick leave from work had already been seriously depleted by all our consultation appointments and would be completely exhausted by the surgery itself. Furthermore, the general surgeon, who would perform the mastectomy prior to the cosmetic phase of the surgery, expressed fear that the abdominal flap could mask recurrence of the cancer on the chest wall. His reservations "tipped the scale" in favor of a silicone implant, and the decision was sealed when the cosmetic surgeon examined my abdomen as a potential tissue site. My physical-fitness regimen had left it taut and toned and without a superfluous fat layer. He was uncertain whether he could get an adequate amount of tissue to build a match for my healthy breast. His disappointment was reflected in his good-natured comment, "I could stop a hundred people on the street and not find one abdomen that flat!"

The day of my mastectomy was dreadful. I had been scheduled for an early morning surgery, and so part of my preparation included having nothing to eat or drink after midnight. An unfortunate glitch in the schedule of one of the surgeons delayed my procedure for about eight hours, which took both an emotional and physical toll. Not only did I have to lie in the hospital bed with anxiety mounting about my pending fate, but by the time I got into the operating room, I was famished, dehydrated, and, consequently, feeling shaky, clammy, and utterly without physical reserves. The surgery went without a hitch, though, in spite of my low reservoir of strength going into it.

No amount of reading or counseling would have prepared me for the kind of pain I would experience in the days and weeks following my surgery and implant. It was white-hot, searing, and unrelenting. Pain killers only partially camouflaged it and wore off well before another dose was authorized. The cosmetic surgeon and his colleagues had done studies that showed the benefits of immediate massage of breast implants to prevent hardening of the surrounding tissue—a condition that leads to an unnatural, rigid result. So on the first morning just one-half day after my surgery, Dr. S. and surgical interns came to my hospital room to teach me how to properly perform the necessary deep pressure massage.

Even though they had ordered a fresh round of pain killers an hour beforehand in anticipation of the lesson, the pain was unlike any I had ever endured, including childbirth. A description eludes me, although it could not be unlike repeated blows to the chest wall with an axe. I had to repeat this ritual four times a day.

So as not to have impaired mobility of the arm on my surgery side, it was also important to begin arm exercises as soon as possible. To that end, on the third day a "Reach to Recovery" volunteer visited me in the hospital to teach me the prescribed regimen of exercises: primarily ball-squeezes with the hand and wall walking with the fingertips. The former produced expected muscular ache and fatigue; the latter sent shards of pain down the length of my arm, bringing me to the verge of tears each time I performed it.

Chemotherapy—which had been recommended by most oncologists as adjuvant therapy—became a necessity when the results of my lymph-node dissection were available. Two of eleven nodes tested were positive for cancer, indicating that my disease had spread from the breast into the lymphatic system; chemotherapy was designed to prevent its metastasis to other sites in the body, often the bones or brain.

Even though several antinausea drugs were added to my intravenously administered chemicals of CMF (cytoxin, methotrexate, and five fluoricil), my oncologist was unable to find any combination of drugs to quell the eight to eighteen hours of severe nausea with acute vomiting that followed each of my six treatments. I would wear a comfortable warm-up suit to each treatment—one that I could wear to bed, as the vomiting would begin almost immediately upon arrival at home afterward. Eventually, after a few hours of acute vomiting, my stamina would be so drained that I had to crawl from the bed to and from the bathroom. After two treatments my hair began to fall out, and after the third treatment I was completely bald. I had sallow skin, sunken eyes, and looked much like pictures I had seen of concentration-camp victims. I continued to go to work, taking off three days for each treatment and its aftermath. Since my sick leave was by now completely used up, I paid back the time by working weekends and evenings between treatments.

In my weakened and emotionally drained state, it would have been tempting to convey the responsibility for my recovery into the hands of the medical profession and its potions. But I learned from members of my breast cancer support group that it is important to retain control of one's own healing process. Women—often unaccustomed to focusing on the needs of their husbands and families ahead of their own—can find such self-focus difficult to attain.

Through the support group, I learned the valuable technique of "imagery." Through this process I learned to envision my body as a strong, healthy place where cancer cells were unwelcome visitors to be expunged at all costs. I "adopted" an image from a book on imagery by other cancer survivors: my good cells were "white knights in shining armor" who slew the black-clad, villainous cancer cells and flushed them out of my body via the "rivers" of my bloodstream. I practiced this technique daily.

The face beneath the turbaned head that stared back at me from the mirror during the five months of chemotherapy was not my face but that of my "other" grandmother—not the grandmother that I had lost to breast cancer but, rather, my mother's mother. Grandma S. was a strong German woman whose hard life had robbed her of her beauty but not of her dignity. She had crossed the plains in a covered wagon as a girl, had lived in a sod house with isinglass windows, had survived

Indian raids and South Dakota winters and the Great Depression. She had the stamina of an ox, and I rarely saw her sit down. Until she was in her seventies, she regularly baked bread and mouth-watering pies in a wood cookstove oven without the benefit of a recipe. She had a ready smile and an inextinguishable twinkle in her eye.

"Women–often unaccustomed to focusing on the needs of their husbands and families ahead of their own– can find such self-focus difficult to attain."

I never felt as close to this other grandmother when I was growing up—not because I loved her less but because I did not feel as though I was as special to her. Grandma S. had several granddaughters, whereas Grandma R. had just me in that role. Grandma S. lived across town, whereas Grandma R. lived right next door, where cozy after school chats were the rule rather than the exception, and thus the bonds of closeness were more easily spun between the two of us.

Today, when I look in the mirror, I occasionally glimpse my "other" grandmother's face. Not because the rigors of chemotherapy have prematurely aged me but because now, nine years later and in my middle fifties, my physical resemblance to her has become more pronounced, Middle age has also accentuated my likeness to Grandma S. in nonphysical areas—having a high energy level, being in almost constant motion, having great reserves of stamina, and living life to its fullest in every moment.

When Grandma S. died, my father said of her and of her daughter Myrtle, my mother, "As long as we have Myrtle, we'll always have Mary." I like to think that if Daddy were alive today, he would take the comparison one generation further and say, "As long as we have Ann, we'll always have Mary."

–Ann M. Ridley Butterfield

Name Change

It's just a name.
A name that is
A scar
A brand
A constant reminder
Of pain
Of lies
Of what you hoped
I'd never remember.
Mother once said
Excusing you for something
"He'd walk through fire for you."
I wish you would.
Walk and burn.
As I do.
To reclaim
What I lost
What you stole
I walk through fire
And through deep earth
And under crushing weights of water
Gasping for air
Fighting for the surface.
It's just a name
But it's too heavy
Too much a part
Of what was.
I'm leaving it behind.
I don't want it.
I don't need it.
I refuse to carry it.
I take the burden
Off my shoulders
And let it fall.
Pick it up.
It belongs to you.

– Kathryn Elizabeth Antea

Romeo: I dreamt a dream tonight
Mercutio: And so did I
Romeo: Well, what was yours?
Mercutio: That dreamers often lie
Romeo: In bed asleep, while they do dream things true.
Mercutio: Oh, then, I see Queen Mab hath been with you

—Romeo and Juliet, ACT I, sc.iv

At My Sister's House

I dreamt a dream last night
That my sister and I
Danced in her den to the rhythms of a Dark Man's music,
Defying gravity with our flailing arms and kicking legs
That flew way,
          way over our heads.

Mom sat on the couch
And smiled at us a bewildered and bemused smile.
A smile that asked,
          Was it me who made them?
          Have I made this joy?"

And we danced the answer,
          "No, Mom. We don't think so."

We kicked higher still,
Laughing so hard
That Sis said to me,
"I'm going to pee in my pants if we don't stop."
And I,
Still imitating her olderness said
I would pee in my pants, too.

And we danced and we danced.

Dad, who sat on the couch
Away from Mom,
Old now, not like before
When he could rip a door
Off the hinge that hid
A frightened child,
Scowled a scowl that said,
"Christ Almighty, must you dance
Your Idiot Dance in front of the TV?
Must you interrupt my pleasure?"

Mom got up quickly
To finish cooking at my sister's house.
My father growled a look that said
"You two, leave with her."
And my sister
In her greatest
           greatest
Choreography of peace,
Pushed her hands straight out and kicked ever higher
To say,
"Shut up old man. We will dance until we die."

My sister looked at me then
And I at her
Not stopping,
Dancing for our lives,
    Kicking,
        Flailing,
            Laughing.
Brave. So brave at my sister's house.

– Elizabeth Anne Stolfi

Salt on a Bird's Tail

In December I will have been waiting a year for a new heart disease treatment. It's not a cure, but my doctors tout it as the next-best-thing to alleviate some of the fatigue that comes with my lifelong heart disease—and the only alternative to a heart transplant. When the FDA clears the way and my name comes to the top of the waiting list, my surgeon will use a catheter to implant a tiny steel mechanism into my heart. The doo-dad, as I've taken to calling it, will cover a hole that now allows used and unused blood to mix together. Covering the hole, the doctor says, will keep the fresh and used blood apart. Only the rich, red, oxygen-laden blood will go out to my organs and limbs and skin.

> "While I wait for the procedure, I'm learning to live a more still life."

While I wait for the procedure, I'm learning to live a more still life. I can't be out walking, can't spend the day hopping from errand to errand. I need time alone and quiet, just sitting by the window or lying in bed with the curtains and windows open.

This waiting and gazing lets me see birds pecking their way across the grass. I think of summer days as a child, when Mother would tell us to go put salt on a bird's tail, something which I now know was her way of saying "Get out of my hair!" At the time, though, it seemed like a bidding to do the magical, and an acknowledgement that such a thing was possible.

We figured that it was a straightforward task: You get a box of salt and wait for a bird to come near, sneak up on it, and put the salt on the tail. I suppose we learned quickly enough that things were not so directly accomplished. But we were not disappointed.

Instead, the actual catching of the bird became unimportant—we were overtaken just by the sensations of the yard itself. The smell of leaves, grass, and flowers wafted in humid air. The grass both scratched and cushioned underfoot. All this sneaking up, the holding of breath, created a quietness and made you super-aware of things around you; how quickly and easily something could move—grass blades waving in the breeze, leaves rustling and lightly touching, dirt crunching underfoot.

And it showed the tiny noises that make up silence. With that summer awareness, some sound always pushed through, some light hiss of life going on and on and on. And that not-quiet quietness somehow revealed that if all things made sounds, had textures and smells, and influenced one another, it was possible to blend in with it all. And then you start realizing the sounds that happen inside of you anyway, the blood and heart and breath and you see that quiet isn't lack of sound there, either. Things keep going on and you can be there in the midst of them, all gently rushing around you, allowing you to be bathed in the simple existence of being alive and on Earth.

> *"Things keep going on and you can be there in the midst of them, all gently rushing around you, allowing you to be bathed in the simple existence of being alive and on Earth."*

The sight of those birds in my back yard brings back to me that feeling of happy trust that patience could let me do something so insurmountably delicate. I realize that this is the kind of hope I bring to my waiting now. I do gentle yoga exercises and am aware of my body stretching, my mind slowing with the in and out of deep breathing. I work at my home rather than an office now, and rediscover how a day really sounds: Chirps, rustles, caws, and a few faraway voices of people tending their yards alone. Once more, I realize that stillness is not truly silent, that my sitting only looks motionless.

And so I wait and stay aware. That awareness keeps me healed every day, living a life that must seem small to some but brings back to me the hush of creeping through the grass on a summer day. I keep my own kind of salt box ready. It contains the salt of hope and faith that enough patience and stillness and being aware of life itself will finally change a life. Just like putting salt on a bird's tail.

– *Leah B. Cates*

Sister

As I reach out to women,
friendships to explore,
my fears fight to the surface,
and I step aside in horror.

Which of them will hurt me?
Which will try control?
Which one will go gently
with my vulnerable soul?

And I pray for the courage
to risk the chance to grow.
With the loveliness of woman,
a Sister I get to know.

The gentleness of woman,
She spares me any games.
In honesty She loves me,
teaching me to do the same.

Feminine does not mean hurtful,
as I once was taught to feel.
This my Sister teaches me,
to be Woman is to be real.

– Caryn Summers

If She Could Keep the Sky

from leaking,
its blue skin stretched tight, so that air
precious and good to breathe
would not pour like money
out the holes and away on solar winds.

If she could hold it folded in her hands
the way she cups Earth. If she could stretch out
her long self on the sky, if it would bend
to her curves, the weight
of elbows, shoulders, hips, her heels
roughing the blue,

if she could reach out both hands
and pull together the edges
of its holes as my grandmother darned socks,
handled one by one from the basket;
the darning egg, its smooth bald head
tucked firmly in the toe, in the heel;
and wove a quilt of stitches
like a maddened spider
until the mesh was thicker, stronger
than the sock itself,

if she could do that for the sky,
pull blue silk from her spinnerets
and darn the opening above those snow-
massed poles,
if she would pull the clouds together,
blanket stitch their edges until the holes
had time to heal,

so that one day the sky would hang
smooth again
around the ball we call Earth,
if she would hold the sky, a silken cloth
light as the air we need and spread it
mended, blue from the north
until it covers us safe in her palm.

– CB Follett

Poem Written
in a Foul Mood

Should I tell people that
my father is dead?
Essentially he is,
not as an organism,
but as a father
he's been dead a long time.
People would ask me
"How did he die?"
Answering could be fun.
He choked on the truth.
His penis exploded.
He fell into the stone polisher.
The garden weasel turned on him.
He spontaneously combusted.
I'd like to see that.
I've heard it's quite something.
I'd bring marshmallows
And toast them
While he burned.

– Kathryn Elizabeth Antea

Dear Sarah

November 2

Dear Sarah,

Once again I acknowledge the special place your friendship has held for me these past twenty-three years. Only with you have I been able to share my innermost thoughts, certain of sympathy and advice, without judgement. Since our junior year of high school, you have upheld and encouraged me through difficult times—yet we have been privileged to share such joyous occasions, too. (Remember Gelsey Kirkland's premier as "Giselle" with Baryshnikov? What an awesome experience! And the party at Piotrowski's where we laughed ourselves to tears). And the loves and trials of our lives, the ecstasies and despairs which have marked our faces with experience and our characters with the stamps which have affected our decisions and choices.

I have yet another burden to share with you. The outcome of this one is yet to be determined. I almost hesitate to put it into writing lest I give it power and alter my fate irrevocably. I have a lump in my breast—following a diagnostic mammogram, the doctor has conservatively guessed that it does not look cancerous. However, it is too small to tell, too small for a biopsy, short of surgically removing it. And it can always become cancerous.

My first reaction is Why? Since I believe that no illness comes to us accidentally, that our lifestyles create the setting, even inviting the illness, I have done considerable soul-searching to understand the source of the problem. Did I place myself under too much stress in my failed marriage? The emotional burden and his alcoholism had become insupportable but did I wait too long to leave? Have I repeatedly "sought" work situations which, initially, seemed beneficial but later turned out to be run by patronizing men more interested in their own aggrandizement than in the efficient running of the organization? Have I suppressed my female strengths, subordinated the woman, the intuition, the caring qualities I possess to compete in the male dominated business world? I've done that twice

43

now in work situations... there's a lesson in there somewhere. So I've turned to meditation and have begun my spiritual quest in earnest. I hope I have time to make some headway.

Still, I have fears about death, about pain. I'm not sure which bothers me the most. If it is cancer, how painful is the experience? Is the pain constant? Does it get worse as it progresses? I would think it does. Or would I just get weaker and weaker until I am too tired to fight? I'm not sure that I fear/resist death so much as that I resent having my life cut short. How much time would I have? Some say there is a chance of living from 5 to 10 years after a bout of breast cancer. That is a small period of time compared with what I wish to do. Everything takes so much time! There is so much left to do, to experience, to feel— I had hoped to love again. When I was undergoing the first tests on the lump, I had this crazy desire to throw myself into an affair–with whom I don't know, that was not the issue–just to have the experience of physical affection and appreciation while I was still "whole." Once surgically cut, I would no longer be "untouched." I would have scars, invasions to remember, a sort of "lost virginity." Not that I could not or would not be loveable again but I would not have the smoothness to my skin—it would be marred by the surgeon's knife. There would be a faint ripple and discoloration there; a visual memory of fear.

Somehow it is different when an accident causes a tear in the skin, a cut somewhere. When you make the decision to have surgery there is something deliberate, calculating about breaking through the skin. Sometimes I awake in the night cradling that breast as if to protect it from harm—from myself? From the doctors? What will protect me from the lump?

I have been fortunate to find a doctor, Dr. John, a holistic practitioner, who is supportive of helping me to find a path comfortable to me, without placing my life in jeopardy. As you know, with the holistic approach, the whole body is treated for the ailment, not merely the symptoms or the single organ. The interconnectedness is important to consider.

John is very attuned to this view of medical treatment. He is our age, a kindred spirit with wonderful, penetrating hazel eyes as if he looks into my soul for the answers. There is a peacefulness, a gentleness about him that instills calm in me, even in the face of the unknown. We wait and watch together. I feel a sense of trust in him, especially when I voiced my aversion to surgery as the answer and he replied, "Surgery is an invasion of the body!" He is helpful in working with me to search for the emotional source of the lump. He, too, believes in the mirroring of unresolved emotion manifesting in the disease of the body. Only this time it is my body with disease. At least we can talk together on several levels, the physical, spiritual, and emotional, knowing that all levels are linked. He does not tell me what to do. We discuss and search together for the answers.

I also have an instinctive repulsion to surgery, the intrusion of the body, the sterility of the operating room with its white tile walls and cold steel instruments. The faceless doctors enshrouded in green converging upon me as I lay strapped and helpless on the table.

A close friend from work recently had the same problem. She quickly turned to the surgeon and had the offending mass removed. She has shared some of the physical aspects of the experience with me—the fact that her surgery was done in an all male setting disturbed her, especially as this is a predominantly female problem. There was no female energy or sympathy in the room for her to find support. Also, she learned later that the reason her ribs and chest cavity were so sore was that, as soon as she was under the effect of the anesthetic, the surgical team forced tubes down her throat, triggering the spasmodic responses of her body to reject these foreign objects. Talk about invasion of the body! She sensed a nameless fear throughout the ordeal, and then had to delay going home for some hours as she was retching repeatedly from the anesthetic. She had not eaten since the evening before, so there was a constant strain on her system to reject what was no longer present. The nausea did not leave her until the following day.

Please keep me in your prayers. I need your support and guidance from the Universe on what my next step should be.

December 6

Dear Sarah,

The lump has grown larger. It is not physically visible, but it is there. The most impossible part of this situation is that medical technology can recommend 1) aspiration of the lump if it is a cyst (invading the cyst with a needle and drawing out the fluid); 2) surgical removal; 3) abstaining from caffeine; and 4) doing nothing but waiting and watching, as it might go away by itself. There is no treatment to help reduce this strange growth within my body. However, I have been using an old folk remedy, castor oil packs applied with heat for one hour daily to the affected area. Occasionally I wonder if it is encouraging the growth of the lump, or if it will reverse the situation if I persist long enough.

Thank you for your kind letter. Only you would contact Silent Unity to add me to their prayer list. Your intuition is so supportive—I feel better since you sense that I am not in grave danger. Your understanding and perceptions seem very accurate to me, especially your remark that I am bringing the whole range of emotions and karmic repercussions of the last decade into balance— if I treat this as a lesson and not simply as an illness. That feels correct to me on a soul level. If only I could stay at that level.

I have begun acupuncture in hopes of triggering the body's immune system to take charge of this foreign body, trapping it and shrinking it into nothingness. I have been taking Chinese herbs. My herbalist, Alan, has recommended certain combinations that will help to detoxify my system and to reduce the risk of cancerous cells developing. Alan also, is of like mind in thinking that the body reflects suppressed emotion if it is not released.

Alan is a very caring, sympathetic man who has dedicated his life to healing and helping others. He has been working with me to build up my physical body with the herbs. It will take about three months before the herbs have had time to start to take effect. It all takes SO long!

I feel positive about taking control of my health. But there is a small voice that asks, "What if it doesn't work? What then?" The small voice is FEAR. Fortunately, there is another, stronger voice, which helps to guide me. I listen to and follow my intuition as much as possible. But sometimes the Fear voice gets very loud.

I have had nightmares of taking off my clothes, looking in my bathroom mirror, and finding one breast has been sheered off. There is a flat, disfiguring scar, much as a large burned area might look. I awake in a cold sweat, shaking and crying. The waiting is almost worse than succumbing to surgery. I vacillate between staying with the long term waiting and watching, acupuncture, and castor oil packs, and with excising the lump from my system and "getting on with" the healing. The main concern there is that, until I identify the source, I am susceptible to more lumps. Many women have faced repeated lumps, repeated surgeries, with no real clue as to the causes.

I am scheduled for more tests in early February. This is supposed to yield more information, although I cannot see what more they will know since the tests are the same as before. Is it that the doctors don't know what to do next? So they stall for time, run more tests, deliberate, and eventually, finally, at last perform the exorcism upon me to remove the lump to decide what it is? And if it's cancer, what then?

I still tend to look at this from an intellectual point of view; part of me is afraid to allow my emotions to enter in as I might fall apart. The first acupuncture treatment with John shook me up. There really was no pain involved, but I trembled for most of the session and burst into tears at the insertion of the third needle (into the top of my foot). Again, it was not from physical pain, but the needles must have triggered feelings which I have been suppressing in order to "survive." John was so caring; he brushed my hair back from my face, took my face in his hands and smiled, looking into my eyes. Then he said, "Isn't God wonderful?" It had an amazing calming effect on me. Although the tears continued to flow, there was not the sense of fear attached. His sense of humor also helped me. I asked him if this emotional outburst was normal for an acupuncture treatment. He smiled and said, "My dear, for you this is as normal as it gets." These pockets of special moments did help me to find value in the lump, for if I did not have it, I would not have sought out such special people as Alan and John.

Yet trying to maintain calm in the everyday experience of work, social interaction, shopping, exercise, means that I have separated myself into parts: one part opens the box and looks at the FEAR and the LUMP; the other part deals mechanically with daily routine; another part allows feeling and spiritual awareness. I need to combine all the areas to fully experience the NOW. But how? It still feels too risky to let more than a little of the FEAR out at any time. I wish there was someone in my life, someone strong and caring, who would hold me and protect me, at least through my tears.

In spite of my years of connection to the Church, I have found no solace there, no spiritual inspiration. All the claptrap of Sunday religion, the Bible quoting and sin-redemption approach, just turn my blood to cold water. I cannot share my fears and doubts with the pastor—his level of sympathy does not extend to women's needs. He still views them through tinted glass.

January 5
Dear Sarah,

Your Christmas card and lovely silk scarf were the perfect treats to lift my spirits. You have such a wonderful sense of color —and your taste is impeccable! Of course, the scarf matches several outfits in my closet.

I'm very sorry we did not have an opportunity to get together. Perhaps we can take a week's vacation somewhere. Sedona would be a restful, restorative place to visit.

I've been using your guidelines for the castor oil packs, envisioning the lump becoming smaller, smaller. Imagination is half the cure! The risk is that my imagination is equally powerful when it comes to fearful images. I must get control of my mind.

Not much more to tell since my last epistle—another mammogram is scheduled for February 4. I, and the doctors, should know more then.

Thank you for your messages of caring and support. If you weren't there, I would be bent under the weight of this. Somehow our spiritual connection has been as pillars to my soul through this. I hope that I will never need to repay your kindness with you facing such an ordeal. Take care.

February 8
Dearest Sarah,

This week has yielded up some wonderful news! I had my second mammogram, followed by an ultra-sound treatment for more indepth diagnosis. The ultra-sound was required after the mammogram showed no more than it did the first time. The lump is not only smaller now, but the doctor was able to tell me that the lump is nothing more than an inflamed glandular mass, a swollen lymph node, most likely triggered by caffeine. I had recently identified an unknown source of caffeine in my diet—Excedrin—which will no longer be in my medicine cabinet. I will have to find another solution for my occasional stress head-aches. Apparently my body is susceptible to the effects of caffeine, more so than most people. Hence, the lump.

I have worked more on unearthing past angers and fears. I seem to have a deep well of sorrow, unidentified as yet, although it has strong links to my inner child. When I am more ready to deal with it, more information will surface, I'm sure. At least I feel headed in the right direction. I hope to start working with a Pathwork counselor next month. They are trained to search for the hidden emotions and help to bring them to the light where they can be dealt with and diffused. I am anxious, yet fearful, to begin.

I am learning to appreciate my lump for the wonderful people it has brought into my life. John and Alan have been a tremendous help to me emotionally and, I hope, physically. I feel very cared for and nurtured. I likely would not have known them, or at least not as well, without this lump and all of the turmoil which has resulted from it. Thank you, lump. Alan has told me to love the lump as my body produced it for a reason. I begin to see his meaning.

March 28
Dear Sarah,

I can hardly believe it, but the lump is gone! Almost as quickly as it appeared it vanished. I have been faithfully using the herbs, the packs, the soul-searching. All of it had a part in my healing, which is still ongoing.

When I told John on my last visit, he was visibly moved and offered a prayer of thanks. I'm still in disbelief. The superstitious part of me will continue the herbs and the packs for a time to insure that the glandular irritation is gone, without chance for a relapse. As John remarked, now the heat is off and I can pursue my spiritual journey with less distraction.

This has been a life-changing experience for me —I hope I shall not backslide into old habits and patterns. I cannot risk my emotional or physical health by following the same old path. I feel sorrow for what my lifestyle has done to my body; yet I have gained valuable insights from this lesson. It will still take some time for me to digest all of this and to find the proper balance in my life.

I still look towards a teaching job in the fall, if all goes according to plan. I have been busy with resumes and letters of application. If I hear from one of the colleges soon enough, I may spend an extra week resting before taking on the new demands of the classroom.

Are you still interested in spending a week at Virginia Beach? I would love to join you. Let me know ahead of time so that I may put in for the time off. I don't mind driving. I can pick you up on a Friday after work to give us a head start. The break will do us both a world of good. I hadn't realized how heavily this illness had weighed on my mind. It is a relief to be on the road to recovery.

That exhibit of the Impressionists sounds lovely. I should be able to make it out for a Saturday, perhaps even Friday evening to get a lead start on the gallery. Maybe we can make a day of it, ending with dinner at the Lebanese Taverna — they have such wonderful food, and the waiters are the best looking men in Washington!

Please remember me to your folks. They are such special people. I'll call you soon.

– Neva A. Clayton

The Woman That I Am

I think the problem is—
when you make love to me, you see me forever young.
"The breasts of a 14-year old," you say.
I wonder if you see the Woman that I am —
Full, wise, mature and real?

My breasts have fed two children.
My womb has seen abuse and disease.
My soul has experienced youth, and is now older.
Wise beyond age, gaining wisdom from mistakes,
I am full and complete.

I do not dance a dance of innocence,
I participate in the celebration of time
I ache to be loved completely,
not in youth but in totality —
Without an expectation of newness.

I am a woman who has come of age.
I hold less tolerance for repetition of mistakes.
Respect the limit of my tolerance.
It is all that I have.
Maturity has removed the rest.

– Caryn Summers

The Feminine

"The image of God as male was at once the most obvious and the most subtle sexist influence in religion...Women were told that God transcends sexuality and were advised not to bother with the trivial question of language."

– Carol P. Christ & Judith Plaskow, *WomanSpirit Rising*

The writers in this section speak both of Mother Earth and the Virgin Mary, knowing intimately that from the wound will arise the ultimate connection to the feminine. The quote above from *WomanSpirit Rising*, presents a common ground for spiritual feminists, no matter what they call themselves—Pagan, Goddess-worshipper, Wiccan, Eco-feminist, Witch. This common ground I can sum up concisely: If language is such a trivial question when referring to God, why does the word, "Goddess" bother so many God-worshippers?

As Z. Budapest very pointedly said, "Goddess kicks butt." The image of a Goddess turns the patriarchal view of the world upside down, challenges it, and redresses it. Some of the words of the writers in this section may unnerve you—for they speak of actually loving our thighs, stomachs, and breasts, holding them sacred instead of longing to have boy-thin bodies. They speak of the aging process as being a time of wisdom, a time of celebration. They honor the feminine.

> *We are the gatherers*
> *We women of all time*
> *We are the singers and the players*
> *Making staccato steps into history*
> *And out again.*

from *The Moon Cries Back*
by Mary Diane Hausman

Not One of Those Girls

I'm not one of those girls you'd call Babe
or dare to lay on your sweet talk,

not one of those girls who thinks the word
lady connotes anything I ever want to be,
who thinks cucumber sandwiches with their
crusts cut off are part of the basic food groups
and I'm not one to let him get away with talking
about the *men* and *girls* at his office,

and yet, girl is what I am after all
with my feet bare and clothes not quite matching, girl
with a good pocket in my fielder's mitt, girl
of trees and ice castles, of an inside curve
and still the girl who wore her first strapless gown
like an erector set with the little bolts missing
from strategic connections.

I'm not one of those girls who lunch, and bid game
while discussing recipes, not one who settles for the
doctor's *"There, there dear, don't you worry about it,"*
but I'm still a girl who's about thirty years younger than
I've aged to, who carries the eight-year-old and sixteen
and twenty-seven-year-old as friend of the heart,

and I'm one of those girls whose bones creak,
who begins to acknowledge the fine hand of time
that jerks the body around to remind us
no matter how much we remain one of those girls,
parts of us need more oil than they used to.

I was not one of those girls who listened
to her mother, but snuck out and walked
in the cool breezes of midnight along roads ending
in country, wind stirring the scent of newly opened maple,

and I'm still the girl who got scared of distance
and shadow but kept walking,
and when I got home, I was the girl
who listened to the wringing of mother's hands
and knew I would go again.

– CB Follett

The Moon Cries Back

There is unity in the chaos
Though we see it not.
It is the invisible fiber of our skirts
Flowing out from legs standing in the field
Gathering cotton, or wheat, or corn.

We are the gatherers
We women of all time
We are the singers and the players
Making staccato steps into history
And out again;

Leaping across dry beds of worn worry
Hoping to find waters to fill our need
As well as earthenware pots
We balance on our heads
As our feet touch down on raw earth.

We walk lands of questions
While answers grow dust on our window sills.
And out of our community of pain
We wail our sorrows to the moon
And the moon cries back:

    The only unity is you
    The only chaos is you
    You, Woman, must come from the East
    You, Woman, must come the South
    You, Woman, must come from the West
    You, Woman, must come from the North
    Come from Above
    From Below
    And from In Between

    Gather yourselves on Sacred Ground
    Spread like the cotton
    Sway like the wheat
    Grow like the corn
    Weave the fiber that spans the Distance
    That makes you Whole
    That make us One.

– Mary Diane Hausman

Stalking the Goddess

I waited for the feminine
creator of love, hope and joy
to manifest herself to me,
but all she did was dictate
another cryptic poem
about some horrible pit
she brought me out of
after hearing my cries.

Though I accept my destiny
like rock turned into lava,
please understand, Goddess,
only my deviant path
led me to your window,
brought me out of that pit.

– Joanne Seltzer

Remembering Brigid

O Brigid
Lady of the Flame,
I have stood
in the fire pit
once your temple;
Touched the walls
of the cathedral
in Kildare;
Heard your name
ringing on the damp
Irish wind;
Felt your sorrow,
cold as stone,
hot as molten iron;
seen you standing
in the mists
arms as wide as earth.
Once a Goddess,
now a saint.
You are remembered
with passion and poetry,
home and hearth,
fertility and fecundity.
Show me, o show me
how to honor you,
graced as I am
by knowing you.

– Mollie Cox Bryan

Poem to the Blessed Virgin Mary

Blessed Virgin Mary, I'm coming full circle, and
I want to be your...what is it I want?
I want to be your child and friend.
May I, again?

Of course, dear Mary, I'd be delighted.
I've missed you.
But first let me ask you
Never to call me by that name again.
I never was a virgin.
Well, of course, I was till the Spring I turned fourteen.
Then sex amazed me.
By sixteen it brought me right into the skies,
Into the eyes of God.
You know, that shattering sweet white light
You want to last forever.
I was lucky with Joseph.
(Older men have some advantages.)
A pity I couldn't tell my friends about it.
They were too busy pricking their fingers
        sewing through hard leather,
To listen to my unbelievable joy.

Now for all this time I haven't told a soul.
Today, I'm telling you, Honey, my child and friend,
        my namesake.
I've kept this secret for two thousand years, Mary:
I loved sex.

– Mary Feagan

Reflections From A Holy Place

Look for the familiar
Touch the holy

There is healing
In touching the sacred.

Mary left her mark
Bcause she
Dared to
Open herself
To the Divine

And if we come
From that Holy Sacred Center
Ma, Mother, Maia,
We are already
Divine

The only redemption
We need
Is to become the Void
Of our own pain

To feel the pull
Once again of
That sacred cord
That holds us
In a great womb
Of flowing power
In the arms
Of Kali-Ma

Without meeting
The Destroyer
We cannot meet
The Life-Bringer

We flow out from
Darkness On
sacred red waters;

We are borne on
Lotus petals
And lilies;
We rise,
Dakinis
Skywalkers.

We walk the face of Ma
And looking in Her
Shining waters,
We see the face
Looking back

Is Our Own

– Mary Diane Hausman

Venus of Willendorf

Though you can cup her in your palm
you could not hold her
if your hands were continents.
She is river beds
and the rolling of foothills.

I say to you, those are hips
to birth a world; like
wind-carved rock receives
the mountain gods and shouts.

She is thighs
and breasts flowing into them,
milk that pulls us into life, carries us
from the dark places of safety
from the dark places of light.

Feel her warm your hand,
the hot transfer of rock into bone.
Long wombed in Earth,
smoke and fire in the wolf night.

How did we turn from the pomegranate,
shed fullness
from our woman-bones,
strive for boy-thin hips, deny our thighs,
reduce our breasts, when all this time
she waited to be found?

– CB Follett

She

She stood on the outside of the Circle, aware that She was different from the people who danced. On the outside She watched.

With Sun overhead, She watched many dances that day. Alone and learning, She listened to good songs. In her quest to understand herself, the woman stood on the outside looking in. Like a lone wolf, She watched and listened and waited.

Sun journeyed West. A good strong drum began to play. It was different than the one before. Yet, the voices were still strong and confident. Clear and pulsating. The Elder announced an Intertribal, announced that all could dance. Part of the young woman wanted to dance. But part of her wanted to stay there—on the outside, safe, not connected. Watching. Listening. Waiting.

Like looking for her own ancestry, She walked to a spot with a good view, distanced from the pulse. Like her own uncertainty, She settled herself on cool Earth with her back against a familiar tree, watching an unfamiliar dance. Listening to the outer sounds with her keen ear, She did not listen to her own strong voice.

Again the Elder encouraged all to dance. Never having danced this way, She was afraid to join others whose movements were easy. She watched as their feet touched the ground lightly, rhythmically. Their subtle movements made the dance look easy, yet She knew it would be difficult. Difficult to let go of her rigid self. Difficult to allow the beat to enter her, even as it now entered them. Difficult to let go of what She thought the dance should be. Difficult to let go of what She thought She should be.

Blue became gray. Still sitting in her comfortable spot on the easy slope leading down to the arbor, She watched as others joined the Circle. People from other tribes danced the Intertribals. White, Yellow, Black, and Red people from around the world all joyously entered the arbor, glad to be connecting with the relatives. From her view, She felt curious of their bond. She watched them move over the Earth, on the lap of their mother. Still, on the outside She remained. Watching. Listening. Waiting.

Then She looked West, discovering what She had been waiting for. In the quiet moments of Sun disappearing, She finally understood. Her ancestors had journeyed West, just as She now looked West. West was the direction of all. And it led her to her Self in her darkened world.

Stars replaced Sun. Finally, the Elder announced that the last Intertribal would be played for the evening. Having finally heard the beat within, She would dance.

> *"Feeling her way into the rhythm, She was at first too excited to understand what She was doing."*

She moved shyly toward the circle. Half walking, half dancing, She moved to the edge. Coyote passed. Eagle flew by. Shawls and feathers. Bells and jingles. Hoops and fans. Differences danced passed her.

Feeling her way into the rhythm, She was at first too excited to understand what She was doing. At first, She was too self-conscious to be aware of the others that joined her. Hesitating inside, the beat reminded her that She was near the edge of letting go. With her beginning steps She was too full at first to empty.

Then draining into Earth Mother, her foot felt the strong beat. It was her beat, her Grandmother's beat, her relatives' beat. It was the beat of all. Without thinking, She, too, became the prayer of the dance.

The young woman felt her back straighten. She felt the power of Earth Mother enter her from below. She felt the rhythm match her heart. She began to empty. She began to join.

Carrying herself with pride, respect moved her steps. With dignity She connected to this great gift. An Eagle whistle blew and She was caught up in a wave of spiritual energy. Moving her. Carrying her. Honoring the young woman, it lifted her as though She were wings.

Filling up with life and living, melting into Earth, finding the beat, honoring all that circles the endlessness, She was truly part of the circle.

Dancing, She looked over to the tree where She had waited. She noticed that the circle extended out past the dance arbor to those that stood on the edges looking in. And like rings in the water's surface, the hoop circled out further and further, to the very edge of her view. Inside and outside, the woman understood that She was always part of the Sacred Circle that She now danced.

– Gina Jones

Wrapped in Moonlight

Had a cup of tea with the Moon Lady, white
elegant, soft, shining, and full. Unbridled.
Her silver-electric waves filled my heart with
Nourishment. Substance.

Felt the pull of Her and the heights of Her as
I was—naked, hungry, and weary from the
sun's relentlessness of its dry, distilled, heat.
Pounding and beating.

Have your golden sunlight while I worship the
Moon in her coal-blue robes of nightsky, jeweled in
Stars, reflecting light in the teacup holding
warmth, wrapped in moonlight.

– Mollie Cox Bryan

Ini Naon Win: Silent Woman

silent child, silent woman
Passing from one into
The other, spanning years

fearful yet Exuberant
pained yet Frolicking
silent yet Boisterous

A dichotomy in a childhood
Of silent emotions passing
hidden into outward frivolity

Slipping silently through
Adolescence into womanhood
The chest-filled silence grows

Ini Naon Win I become
Through wifehood, motherhood
Body expands to hold its growth

Middle-agehood envelops child
Sisterwoman opens the gilded chest
Tsunami of emotions explodes

Ferociously cleansing the past
Washing out to a sea of tranquility
Leaving the gilded chest empty

Ini Naon Win seeks to fill it
silence slithers in stealthily
To fill the aching emptiness

Awake, silent one, to the danger
Guard against this lurking past
Keep the chest clean, love-filled

Fill the void with Earth Mother
Sage and cedar to cleanse
Flutes, flowers and Red Road

From childhood to womanhood
Ini Naon Win is created
Passing silently into Spirit Woman.

–Virginia Butchart Cowie

Note: Ini Naon Win means "silent woman" in the
Dakota language.

Wisdom Women

Old women, you were the lattice
for new growing vines, used to tell
how fire was kindled, blazed,
how the years turned and seasons
swelled with new growth.

Dark eyes nearly hidden
you kept the secrets. Waited.
Planned when to fish, plant,
harvest the tall grain. You
instructed girls in the mysteries

of blood and sex,
birth, children. You held the moon
on a silken thread, tugged it
around the Earth so cycles interwove

with songs you sang by dark-night
while the moon slept, the sky lit
with thousands of stone fires.
You chanted our histories,
how we moved

across land and stream bed to come here,
and when we moved from here, as spring
heated the land, this too would you braid
into the story, spinning it out
in thick plaits.

Now, old women don't tell us
what is carried in their wisdoms.
They live silently
separate from the rest of us
and the long call of the owl is far.

– CB Follett

After Her Surgeries

What Lima found on the beach
were broken goddesses,
branching bits of coral
suggesting the feminine,
Venus torsos
all minus limbs
or breasts or heads.

Lima stooped to the sand
to study their whitened perfection,
gathered salty goddesses into a pouch,
later gave them to her women friends
to remind them each
of their central divinity,
whatever else may be missing.

– *Connie Hershey*

Spring

Spring is a woman,
who thaws slowly, leaving patches
of snow behind, teasing
with hints of green
and buds that promise
of daffodils, dandelions,
tulips, cherry blossoms—
beauty yet to come.

Her name is Oya. Her rivers
and streams rush, roar, rise,
and flow over rocks, sand, mud,
to kiss all life with wetness,
cool and crisp, driven
from the winter snow.
She gurgles with giggles.

Her name is Gaia. Smell Her
rich, luscious soil. Feel the
contractions from her life-giving
core while she gives birth
to the music of robins,
sparrows, and cardinals.

She labors, toils, and pushes.
She dances, giggles, and flirts.
She is raw beauty.
Her name is Woman

– Mollie Cox Bryan

The Family

I cherish this section. Even as society's definition of family expands and changes, women are usually at the center, holding it together in one way or another. More grandmothers are raising grandchildren. More mothers are raising children alone. More families struggle with poverty, drugs, and violent crime.

In the midst of this turbulent and changing family structure, we forget how much divorce, abuse, and violence hurt. We are too busy clicking our tongues, shaking our heads, and offering judgments. Judgments about same-sex families, multicultural families— any family that may appear different than society's 'norm.'

In this section you will share with the writers who celebrate the strength they find in their families as well as with others who long for refuge from them. They address lesbianism, divorce, dysfunctional families, birth and, yes, even abortion.

> *The images in the mirror surround me*
> *As I comb through the ever shortening strands of time.*
> *A family portrait painted on my face.*
> *Time was my friend when I was a child.*
> *Now it slips away faster than I can think.*
> *I want to linger—to drink in the generations*
> *And hold them—because they*
> *are me.*

from *Family Portrait*
by Cynthia C. Rosso

Labor Day

Martha Miller listened to NPR's *All Things Considered* with one ear. As she emptied the steaming dishwasher, her thoughts were on the weekend's activities. Labor Day weekend had never been that special for her, but today she anticipated her daughter's visit. Laura would be in town for the big Carr's auction. Laura had recently opened Used Wares, an antique shop, in Lakewood, N.J.

Martha's listening quickened when she realized that Lynn Neary was talking about gay rights. All Martha heard was "same gender covenants." "What church? What state?" she mentally screamed.

Martha turned off the radio when the phone rang. Joan called to report on the demonstration at the Board of Education for free condom distribution at local high schools. "You would have liked it. Maybe a hundred people against and sixty of us for. Your odds. Several teachers from T. J. High School asked about you," Joan rattled barely saying hello. "I told them you were happy in retirement. After twenty years as a high school social worker you need vegging-out time."

"I'm glad to know I was missed," Martha responded. "But I'm glad I didn't fit it into my day. I enjoyed getting ready for Laura. Anyway, I'll be going with you next week to Richmond for the Children's Rights March."

After Joan's phone call, Martha decided to wait for Laura on the deck. The warm, fresh air enhanced her upbeat attitude. The high constant chirping of the tree frogs made her smile. "Wonder what their gossip is tonight?"

The jarring slam of a car door and a second more muffled slam brought Martha from her musings. She heard the two women laugh. Startled, she felt a slight chill. The laughter seemed to silence even the frogs for a moment.

Martha hurried to the driveway. Talking and smiling, Laura and her friend were walking toward the house arm in arm. "I'm glad she has a close friend," Martha thought. Laura had not brought any friends home during the 18 months she worked at Christie's in New York City. Martha had worried about Laura then.

Martha and Laura separated from their hug. "Mom, I want you to meet Heidi. Heidi, this is my mom. I'm sure that my two favorite women will get along great," Martha gave Heidi a cordial hug.

Luggage in. Port poured. The three women talked about the trip. Laura handed Heidi a small mound of pistachios she had shelled. This was Heidi's first trip to D.C. She wanted to know how best to spend her few days. Amid the light talk and laughter Martha felt joy, pride, and love. "I want to be at Carr's preview by ten." Laura said, "Bedtime."

Martha did not go to sleep immediately after going to bed. Something vague bothered her. "Probably too much port, too late," she thought.

"Yuk, drizzly, misty rain." Laura grumbled to Martha as she poured her breakfast coffee.

"You were born on a day like this so I rather like this weather," Martha responded. The sleepy expression on Laura's face made Martha realize that conversation should be postponed awhile.

As Heidi walked into the room a few minutes later, Laura immediately brightened. Smiling she said, "We have a choice of cereals, muffins, and fruit. Tomorrow morning, when we have more time I'll make my famous omelets."

"Mom, would you drive Heidi into town and I'll meet her after I'm finished at the preview?"

"Sure. Will you be back for dinner? I have a ham and homemade potato salad."

"Sounds good. I'll call when I know what time we'll be home."

"Have a great day, bye." Martha called to her daughter. Then to Heidi she said, "As soon as you're ready, I am."

"Great," said Heidi. "Looks like the rain will stop soon. I'm sure things will clear up."

During the forty minute ride to the Air and Space Museum, Martha learned that Heidi was the oldest of three daughters. Her father and mother were school teachers in Michigan. With a masters in math from the University of Michigan, she became a stock analyst because the money was good. She and Laura had met singing at the Gilbert and Sullivan Choral Arts Society.

As Heidi got ready to leave the car, Martha noticed the bracelet she wore. "That gold bracelet is stunning."

Heidi said, "Laura gave me this. Thanks for the ride. See you this evening."

Throughout the day Martha replayed the morning's conversation several times. Something about Laura and Heidi's relationship was puzzling. There was nothing about Heidi to dislike. What was annoying her? "I don't remember reacting to any other of my children's friends this way. Could I be jealous of Heidi? Why? They certainly like each other." Such thoughts kept circling through her mind. By 3:30 p.m., Martha's head was pounding. She took two Tylenols, a hot shower, and went to bed.

When Laura called about 6:00 p.m., Martha woke alert and clearheaded. Laura and Heidi would return by 7:30 p.m. Martha had ample time to dress and get dinner ready.

Hearing the car, Martha went to the kitchen window to study the two smartly dressed young women. They were talking, one head with a long blond braid and one head with loosely curled brown hair nodding to each other. "My mother would have enjoyed them," she thought. "Of course, my mother would have been worried that they are almost thirty and not married. Women today don't need men like we were taught to. What a gift to be allowed freedom to pursue one's own dreams instead of society's." Martha was suddenly filled with the awareness of how proud she was of Laura and how deeply she loved her.

Dinner was a chaotic exchange of the day's activities. Using a French accent, Laura told about meeting an antique dealer from Quebec who said he had to come to D.C. to find French antiques because in Canada anything made from wood gets burned in cold weather. Heidi related the actions of a security guard and lost German shepherd in the Natural History Museum. She said that at times she thought the guard was the one who was lost. He had to keep looking at his map. Martha told them about Laura's French poodle who used to follow her to grade school often making her late for school. Sometimes the three women all talked at once. Laughter was abundant.

Around midnight, they decided to call it a night. Just before Martha turned off the lights, she noticed Laura's jewelry on the kitchen counter. "This bracelet is similar to the one I noticed on Heidi. No. It is the same bracelet." She turned the bracelet in her hand, noticing the engraving— "L., all my love forever H." She reread the inscription, put the jewelry down, and shut off the lights.

After a few sleepless hours in bed, Martha took two Nytols and drifted into a fitful sleep.

Opening one eye at a time, Martha saw her daughter's smile. She mumbled, "Thanks for the juice. Be in the kitchen in a minute."

At the kitchen table Martha took a much needed sip of coffee. "Do you like the coffee? I found this delightful gourmet place about two blocks from my shop. Sometimes we walk there after supper," Laura said as she did the final fold on the omelet.

"It's good." Martha took a large swallow. Paused briefly, then continued. "When you say 'we' walk after supper? Is there someone special in your life?" She wasn't sure she wanted an answer to that question. "Please God" she prayed, silently "let the someone be a man."

Laura carefully placed the omelet garnished with some fresh fruit in front of her mother, poured herself more coffee, then sat down. "I guess mothers always know. Yes, there is someone special in my life," Laura answered.

"I've had a roommate for several months now. I am sure that this will be a long-term relationship. Before I upset you with this arrangement, I wanted to be sure myself." Laura paused for a reaction from her mother.

"I appreciate your consideration. You know I will always love you. You also know that although I do not agree with the idea of 'living together,' it is what many young people do. I won't condemn it either." Martha phrased her words carefully.

"Mom we are in love." Laura's eyes were getting misty as though tears might start soon.

Martha had no choice. She had to help her daughter.

With her fork halfway to her mouth she heard herself ask, "Is it Heidi?"

Laura took a deep breath, exhaled and looked directly into her mother's eyes. She nodded and said "Yes."

Martha was suddenly numb, cold. Maybe if she said something she would awaken from a bad dream. Finally she said, "Good omelet. You haven't lost your touch."

"Mom, you are so wonderful. I thought you would understand."

"No. I don't understand. I have lots of questions, but I can't even begin to articulate them. I'm taking a shower. Have a good day." Martha paced each word.

Martha turned on the shower, sat on the commode, and began to cry. She cried for a long time. By the time she stepped into the shower the hot water was gone. She went to her bedroom to wait for the tank to reheat.

What went wrong? In high school she had lots of boyfriends. She went to her prom. She looked so beautiful that night....She didn't play with dolls as much as some girls seem to. She liked her brothers' cars and puzzles a lot....Most girls went to school in slacks....She liked being in the kitchen with me.

As she felt the warm shower, Martha said to herself, *Okay, if I were counseling another mother in this situation, what would I say? I would somehow ask her what she was afraid of. I don't want my daughter to be a lesbian.*

After she got dressed, Martha tried writing her thoughts, fears, and solutions. How would her sons react? I can hear the grandchildren. *'Why is it Aunt Laura and Aunt Heidi? Shouldn't it be Uncle Heidi?' My brother will say all my children are strange. My sisters will arrogantly agree that I should be pitied, then proceed to discuss their daughters' weddings. I remember the first time I held Laura. I thought of all the pain and joy she would have. I thought her wedding would be one of the joys.*

Martha's thoughts never got to the paper.

The house was beginning to close in on her. Martha needed fresh air. As she started to walk, she also started to relax. She looked at her neighbors' well-maintained houses wondering what was going on inside. Were they laughing or crying? Nearby, brakes screeched. A car stopped just in time to miss a cocker spaniel. Her thoughts went to Laura's reaction to the ordeal of having

Jacques put to sleep. A teenaged couple holding hands, giggling oblivious to everything but each other passed within feet of her. *Love is grand!* She sat down on a rock. She listened to the rustling leaves. She watched the moving shadows of the leaves.

A Pizza Hut delivery car sped by. *Must be getting close to dinner.* Time to go. Lifting herself from her seat, she could feel that her joints had become stiff. Her back hurt. "I used to feel this way when I was nine months pregnant," she sighed.

The red light was blinking on the answering machine when she got home. The recording announced that Laura and Heidi would be back soon with take-out. Martha realized she was hungry.

The couple came in with two bags from Hunana Star. "How was your day, Mom?" Laura asked. Martha just looked at them. Laura continued, "I got some good deals, but I never really know what customers want."

"Sounds good," Martha answered. Talk was stilted and forced. At times during the meal Martha wondered if they were speaking Chinese as well as eating it.

Finally, Laura said, "Mom, we should talk. You must have something to say, some questions."

"I'm not ready yet. Let's just watch the PBS concert tonight."

Martha watched Heidi and Laura as much as she watched TV that night. She saw two people genuinely caring about each other.

"Perhaps, it is love," she mused as she went to bed. "I'd probably like Heidi a great deal if one of the boys had brought her home."

The women were ready to leave by ten the next morning. Each woman hugged Martha to say goodbye. Martha did not want to let Laura go. She knew, however, that she must. "I love you. I'll call soon." Martha said as she did let go.

After she could no longer hear the car, Martha finished getting dressed. As she pulled a sweatshirt from the bottom drawer of her dresser, an envelope fell to the floor. Martha took out the tiny identification band..."BABY MILLER—FEMALE"... the date of birth was indistinct.

– *Salome Harasty*

Grandma Falls Asleep

Vacuum-cleaner lungs suck
Nights in and out
With Both the sensuous and ideal.
Old and new protrude from the ridicules.

The comfort of age comes from
Observing that Nothing from which the Most-Basic runs
A few miles around the track
Into a minute.

Minutes expand.
Bursting buttons off both chest
And bottom, they become years.
Years fill with the sound of small things,
Inexorable and fractious—in celebration of loves and hassles.

Decades stride out of children.
They transform,
Until you see outlined—quite unbelievably—
Your own live locus winging into centuries.

–Joyce Cook

Strong Tea

Three women sit like the Fates, weaving
their families lives, as they sip Constant Comment
from speckled gray-brown mugs.
Spoons fish for spent bags, the fingers find tags
and wrap the muddy stained strings
around the bag, sqeezing the last flavored drop.
The not-quite-silver spoons stir sugar
and clang, clang, clang, ring in their ears—singing
of money, husbands, and children.

Steam floats into the air. Tea-smell comforts
three women around the kitchen table.
Aunt Judy dribbles and giggles.
The room fills with the sound.
Mom and Aunt Mart light-up as they laugh.
Orange and icey-pink lipstick scars
white cigarettes and marks their mugs
with painted lip stain.

Bittersweet tea-tastes linger.
"The stronger the better" they would all say to me
between puffs, songs, and tears.
Their sounds steep into me and fill my cup—
I taste the strength.

– Mollie Cox Bryan

Dialogue with An Inner Wisdom Figure

Sleepy-lidded eyes, Great Cat,
    be with me.
Breathe your engine-panting power into my slack belly,
    belly growing big.
Hips soften now and walk with your special sway,
feet with huge pads sinking, springing walk,
      earth-connected,
the two-feet-below-crushed-fir-floor walk
    so silent, soundless.
Ears move, rotate, flick to be alerted to the tiniest sounds,
    but all is well.
Suddenly, a fly makes the skin and muscles ripple,
    a delicious energy play,
and the fly is displaced.
How easily you rid yourself of irritations and distractions.

Yes, I see.
You save yourself for the big dangers and the giant game.
But you have two mighty weapons,
    your roar for one,
purposeful, powerful, to the point, and true,
    and your great red courage—
a line like an arrow shot straight and unbroken all the way to
    your heart.
Glowing, it warns others not to try going up against you.
    Would-be enemies slink away.

You walk along, peacefully, masterfully in the fullness,
    in the fullness of your power.
Only your tail gives away a certain flicking playfulness.
And now, resting your chin in your paw, tranquility,
    and no where else to be.
From this I sense you to be the gentlest of mothers.
    Be with me, Mama.
Let me know the great courage line to my heart.

– Susan Galbraith

Dreams of Grandma

My dreams are filled with images of my Grandmother. In one, I pick her up and carry her. She is light as a child and cradles herself against me. In another dream, she comes back to her home from the personal care home she lives in now. Looking 20 years younger, she seems so vital and so much the woman I have always known.

Dreams of Grandma are not new to me. She has always been in my life, therefore, she has frequented my dreams from time to time.

My dreams of her now are mostly filled with confusion and pain. Hers, because of the deep soul-seering loss of her mind, which once was sharp and quick. Mine, because I am forced to watch this utter degradation and humiliation of a woman who was once very proud.

I awaken from these dreams early in the morning, feeling a disturbing turbulent mixture of emotions. One second, I cry. The tears just begin and I want to scream from the sweet relief of knowing she is finally being cared for, is safe, warm, clean, and dry. I then think about the dream I've had, try to analyze it. What do these dreams of Grandma mean?

Consulting a psychoanalyst or a dream analyst, I feel, would be cheating myself somehow. I sense that these dreams are a part of the process of coming to terms with the loss of my Grandmother. I need to resolve these images—both the real ones and the dream ones—I have of her, for I really do not know how to keep the older, more vital memories of her alive, while I watch her being taken by Alzheimers.

Grandma was, of course, everything the word "Grandmother" evokes. All and more. Not just Gram, but Irene Violet Snowwhite Carpenter, a "career woman" long before that phrase was ever coined; a devoted Christian and church organist; a patron of the arts (in all forms) and of artists (she even married one); and, at one point in her life, she was even a pilot. Gram was the first woman to ever fly a seaplane.

(I remember asking her once why she was not afraid to fly a plane. She laughed and said of course she was afraid, but "just because you're afraid of something doesn't mean you shouldn't do it").

Born Irene Violet Snowwhite, she grew up a tomboy. Her parents had both grown up as farmers, but did everything from publishing to mail delivery to make a living. Her young world was full of new vehicles called "horseless carriages" and victrolas. Her parents doted on her, yet they were very strict. They provided a safe and overprotective household. When Gram became a teenager she was properly forced to give up her tomboy ways—and she did, but only by appearance. She probably knew nothing about sex, except whatever the preacher sermoned on Sundays against it, the sinfulness of it. Yet, somehow, she became pregnant. I imagine she had no idea what was happening to her or what the lifelong results were to be.

"I need to resolve these images – both the real ones and the dream ones – I have of her, for I really do not know how to keep the older, more vital memories of her alive, while I watch her being taken by Alzheimers."

Nobody in the family seems to know what age she was. We just know that she was a young teenager when it happened. We also know that she began to miscarry. While she laid in bed hemorrhaging, she finally told her parents what happened; her mother wanted to take her to a hospital. Her father, a strict, devout, Presbyterian man, threw a fit and demanded his daughter lie there and suffer and think of her sins. He refused to allow her to go to the hospital, for then it would be common knowledge that she was a "loose" young woman. She stayed home and never properly healed.

A few weeks ago, when my father was visiting Grandma, she told him she was pregnant.

"You know, I'm pregnant," she said. "And if my father finds out, he'll just kill me."

The Alzheimers has continuously taken her back to that traumatic time. She speaks of her father in fearful tones. She also sometimes thinks her current husband is her father. Yet, she still found comfort in knowing her "father" would be with her in the personal care home.

Grandma has also asked me if I knew if the adoption went through.

"Of course, it did Gram. You adopted my Mom. You remember, that red-headed lady..."

"Oh yes," she says and giggles. "How could I forget her?"

She then explains that she and Grandpap tried twice to have their own child. She suffered two horrible miscarriages. Finally, her doctor suggested adoption. I believe that today the doctor would have also asked her to consider a hysterectomy. Since he did not, years later, Grandma suffered and beat ovarian cancer. She only stopped her career long enough to get over the cancer.

She held a job in almost every one of Beaver County's hospitals, even in Sewickley Hospital. She stopped roaming when she got her position at Aliquippa Hospital, where she was Assistant Controller for 22 years. Some of my earliest memories are of playing with the typewriters, adding machines, and the switchboard at the hospital. I also remember when they received their first computer. Gram and I were amazed with the thing. It was huge and noisy and spit out computer cards that I sometimes played with like some girls played with paper dolls or baseball cards. I also remember her getting phone calls any time during the night and early morning hours about some problem at the office. She would get up, drink her coffee, eat her raisin toast, and go to the office—whether it was 10:00 p.m. or 3:00 a.m. No questions asked.

Gram worked hard, but she also played hard. It seemed as if she entertained at least once a month and she used to take off with her women friends to Niagara Falls, Florida, New York City, North Carolina. Grandpap hated to travel so she left him at home. These times of separation were probably a relief to both of them. He was an alcoholic, though then, I think he was just known as a drunk. The disease was not named or understood then. He was probably glad to see her go—he could drink all he wanted, without listening to her bitch about it. And, she was probably tired of bitching, too. Maybe it wasn't the healthiest of reasons to live sort of independent lives, while still being married, but I have taken a great lesson from them. I feel marriage does not have to mean complete interdependence, in fact, I shudder at the thought of a husband who would command me to make my life his. Grandma and Grandpap Carpenter's love for one another was strange in its day, but nonetheless, it endured up to, and beyond, his death.

"It scares me to think that somewhere in her mind she is still that strong woman and is struggling to understand why she can't remember."

I remember Grandpa's wake at her house. I remember watching her smile and entertain that day. When everyone went home, I stayed with her. I sat on the living room sofa. It was blue-green and rough-textured. She went into the back of the trailer home. Out of the quietness, came a cry. I ran to the back—it was Gram in the hallway, holding herself up against the wall, one of her hands on her heart. She was finally crying. I grabbed her around her thighs—I was only seven years old—and hugged them as tight as I could.

"Don't tell anybody," she finally said to me. "Don't tell anybody. Not your mother. Not your Greatgrandma. Don't tell them I've been crying. They would just worry about me. I don't want anybody worrying about me. I'll be all right. I just miss your grandpap. But, I'll be all right."

It scared me to see her cry. I still remember the fear creeping into my belly. At that young age, I had seen my mom cry, and even my father. But, never Gram. I had thought she was perfect, beautiful, invincible. And maybe there's a part of me who still hangs on to that perfect vision of her, which cruelly clashes with the Alzheimer's-ridden woman she is now. It scares me to think that somewhere in her mind she is still that strong woman and is struggling to understand why she can't remember, why she can't understand, why she can't think. It also scares me to think that somewhere in her mind, I may be lost. My love for her may not be remembered now. She sometimes does not even know who I am. I want her to know how much she has meant to me, how much I love her, and how much more I need to learn from her. I do not want her to die in confusion feeling unloved and unneeded.

At the age of 30, while I contemplate my life, my future, having children, becoming a mother, then grandmother, I turn to the woman friend I have always known as my Grandmother, for inspiration, for direction. She did it. She raised a daughter, had a career, and a successful marriage—a full, rich life. How did she do it? I need to know and feel frustrated knowing that she would give me her secret ingredients, if only she could. This, along with all of the other magical secret ingredients she has already given me, would make my life easier to fulfill. Instead, I will have to make my own way.

It intrigues me that Grandma keeps going back to the times of her pregnancies. She also goes back, at times, to her working days, but not as often, nor as vividly. She seems to be reliving her pregnancies. When she speaks of her job, sometimes she remembers real ones; other times, she has taught school or waitressed, neither of which she has ever done. It's almost as if the pregnancies and her adoption of my Mother are the only real substance of her life in her mind. Maybe it is all that really mattered to her as she trudged off to work each day, gallivanted to Chinese restaurants at midnight, took a road trip to Florida, or flew a plane.

I fly through my days at the office, much the same way she did. I tend to go to plays or movies, poetry readings, and Chinese Restaurants. I sometimes vacation without my husband. When I dream of my future, I think of a place in the country, making time for children, gardening, poetry, and, yes, time for flying.

– *Mollie Cox Bryan*

The Family Portrait

In the mirror is a woman I do not know
and yet she is familiar.
She is not the one I saw yesterday
when I was curling my hair.
Her eyes search through the glass at me
As I slip the comb through the graying strands.

She is my mother, rounder than before.
Her shoulders show fatigue
And there is wear around her eyes.
Her hair is tinted to cover white strands,
She stands strong, but alone,
Still looking for love,
But on weary feet.

She is my sister, someone I barely know
but am just discovering as we race toward twilight.
One who bore the pain of loveless years and depression,
Whose hair turned many colors in that time,
But whose hands can create lace
With the ease of the grandmother I never knew
Who taught her how.

She has my daughter's laugh and determination
but the face is so different.
She is dancing although she is not moving.
Her essence says to do it, create it, dream it.
Constricted by her own body,
The dancer does not fade.

I see a child in the mirror—one yet to come.
She's free and laughter bubbles from her lips.
She bounces through fields.
Her shoes are untied and she does not care.
Life is today and it is wondrous.
Tomorrow brings a new adventure
and so does the next.

There's my dad—I almost lost him
But he's standing in the shadows
Just looking at me and smiling.
I become warm in his arms.
He cares for me as for a treasure.
His eyes follow me for he cannot say,
"I love you."

The images in the mirror surround me
As I comb through the ever shortening strands of time.
A family portrait painted on my face.
Time was my friend when I was a child.
Now it slips away faster than I can think.
I want to linger—to drink in the generations
And hold them—because they
are me.

– *Cynthia C. Rosso*

A New Author

(For my Daughter, McKell)

Who she is becoming
has not to do with me.
My lessons have been taught,
good and bad.
The next chapter is hers.

Who she will be tomorrow
is a mystery to me.
I cannot read
what has not yet been written,
and she holds her own pen.

And now it is she
who will turn the pages.
She no longer climbs on my lap
to listen to me read.
It is her own bedtime story now.

She may decide
on a different story than mine,
more adventure than romance,
less poetry, more prose.
I pray she that she likes a happy ending.

– Caryn Summers

Hearing Appalachian Spring When the House is Nearly Empty

They leave all at once in three cars. I pray
for their long absence. Only the dogs
and one sleeping baby remain. Strung out and tired
of tending, I collapse with Copland. The strings
begin softly and barely muffle the howls
of the locked-out Labrador. The bass
advances and I join the celebration—
those Quaker newlyweds
in their housewarming joy, I
in my houseweary cynicism.
They dance in blessed unknowing
with the hope and ignorance
of the newly loved. Staccato
forebodings warn of everyday life.
The red dog barks at a squirrel.

Then enters the old melody, borrowed
hymn to freedom and simplicity. I recall
the old Shaker woman on TV, last
of the celibate last, shining
in her starched white bonnet
as she quavered: "'Tis a gift
to be simple, 'tis a gift to be free..."
Here in this house, solitude
seems the dearest and least simple
gift of all. The music ends.
The black dog unlatches the door.
The waking baby sings.

– Elizabeth Stoessl

Chechnya

More than 500 Russian mothers have removed
their sons from the Chechnya battle. Thousands
are preparing to follow in their footsteps. Dateline: Moscow.

Come with me son. Come
away from these dark fields of blood.
Put down the gun you've never learned to shoot.
Look at me. I gave you life.

My barely raised boy, it was not for this
the water broke, not for this I stood
in lines, knitted mittens and wool caps,
not for this I sharpend Uncle Petyr's skates
for the blue pond ice.

Would I do it for my sons,
go 500 miles to take them from war?
In my heart yes, a million times but my bones
falter.

When they were eighteen I went to meetings
in modest living rooms, to coffee-splattered offices
with fliers on the walls and phone numbers
and tattered articles on young men
being prosecuted for refusing.

I looked for ways into British Columbia, re-examined
my father's Canadian birth. I told them,
you don't have to sign.

Galena travels from Omsk
to take her son from war, finds his troop train
already clattering its way toward Chechnya.
The counselor gets her on the next train.

The smell of mud, motor oil
and soaked bandages. The hive sounds
of bullets flying true and straight,
and Galena's son is stunned to see his mother
talking to soldiers, Mother,
what are you doing? We're fighting.

She drifts through smoke
plucking at sleeves. It's hard to focus
but he sees someone point
and she comes. Do her thick shoes
touch ground; will she fade
if he blinks?

Vladmir, she says, hand gentle
on his arm. Put down the gun.
I didn't feed you to kill.
And she leads him from the battle field.
Who questions a strong woman
you know is right?

I remember them little. How
their bony shoulders softened
when they lifted their arms
to be picked up.

– CB Follett

brief return of the mother

my mother came into my room
still dead from all those years
an odor of dirt and amber
breaking from her
she pointed with slender finger
to all my big ideas
where would you be
without me?

blonde strands of her hair
touched gigantic shoulders
my mother a statue!
I bowed under the shadow
of her hard gown

O mom!
pray to the gods for me
those gods you surely touch
and tell them
for me
I have wandered
I have wandered!

– Su Byron

Gift of Tears

Hurriedly, I prepare for a holiday visit. The three children and I are going to see Mr. B., as we affectionately call him. We want to deliver our gifts and wish him and Mrs. B. Merry Christmas—for the third time. Already these Christmas visits are becoming a kind of tradition, and this year we hang tightly to threads of connection back to happier, calmer days. We feel the happy excitement of anticipation.

The children first met Mr. B. four years ago when he was their crossing guard at the busy corner they had to cross on their way to school. They considered him their third grandpa. I thought he was a retired minister. His silver hair and gentle strength gave him a saintly look. But he also had a streak of Santa in him. Keeping his pockets well stocked with gum, candies, and other small gifts, on the corner he was the children's gift giver, confidant, and friend. When he wasn't chatting with or escorting children across the street, he was busy watching squirrels hide nuts or bluejays chase cats. He was seeing autumn trees drop leaves, children climb snowbanks, or winter turn to warm and glorious spring. For him each season of the year held its own beauty, and every day was full of fresh surprises both for him and for the children he watched over.

One chilly November afternoon after crossing Mr. B.'s corner, Erik came home wearing a new pair of warm maroon gloves. "Where did you get those?" I asked.

"From Mr. B.," he answered. "He felt bad I didn't have any mittens so he bought me some. He thought my hands were cold."

Now four years later his hands and ours *are* cold. The thermometer hovers near zero. The snow and wind blow in and through our small midwestern city. We are cold and alone but we feel Christmasy. Our three small gifts are wrapped —a picture of the children in a small gold frame, a book of Peter Marshall prayers, a green plant. We back safely out of our semi-shoveled driveway and drive carefully and slowly on the ice and snow the five miles to the B.'s small ranch-style home neatly nestled on a small city lot now covered with snow.

Late afternoon excitement and activity welcome us. After the hugs and hellos, Mr. B. measures the children and pencils their end-of-the year heights on the kitchen wall. We compare them with the previous years' marks and agree that the three have grown like midwest weeds. The children go down the hall to pay their annual respects to the teddy bears hibernating in the grown daughter's bedroom. In each room decorations and tiny traditional touches of Christmas fill nooks and crannies of the immaculately groomed home. We carefully look at and examine each thing. Mrs. B. with her quiet dignity and gentle ways prepares and serves treats while Mr. B. reads us *The Grinch Who Stole Christmas*. We sit around the living room listening, sipping grape ice cream sodas, and munching homemade Christmas cookies.

I sit on the soft sofa, my body tired, and my mind drifting in and out of the moment. The warmth of the family home, the silent communication between the aged couple, their care for one another, their love for us, the presence of my three children seated around me—all weave together to fill me with a sense of peace. The spirit of Christmas seems to flow into my heart and very being. I can almost touch it. I want to sit here forever. I've lived in conflict too long. I've forgotten what peace feels like. Now I want to carry it with me always wherever I go, never to lose it again.

Did George really move out of the house less than two months ago? We have separated—for the second time, this separation to lead to divorce. Can it be? Disbelief and thirteen years of memories bury me—a star sapphire engagement ring, a small church wedding on a sunny California day in June, a firstborn son—"He's gorgeous," I'd said, a thesis for George to finish, two beautiful daughters, pails of diapers, colic, and interrupted nights, exhausting days, first steps, a postdoc and a job, four moves, holiday celebrations and family fun, a house and garden, tenure, everything that was supposed to matter, the storybook life. We had it all. Then it all crumbled and the book closed. What happened and why? What did it all mean? Questions, always questions, but never answers. I live numb in confusion.

"Mommy!" The sound of my daughter's voice interrupts my reverie. It is time to go home. I get up from the soft sofa and carry dishes to the kitchen. There on the formica of the kitchen table are two oval Christmas placemats. Lying innocently side by side, they trigger an eruption of emotion. And there in the kitchen I realize—for the first time: "I have no one to grow old with."

We put on our coats, say goodbye, and drive off in the silence of snow. And there in the car in the quiet snowfall at dusk I cry—for the first time. Tears run down my hollow cheeks, washing, cleansing, and loosening the tightness of my tired body. My winter-weary spirit seems to rise and reach for the stars beyond the snowy sky. Peace and gratitude flow in, my mind clears, and I know in my heart that the future will write itself. Growing old will come in its own good time and in its own season. I have today. Tomorrow will come when it is ready, and I need not trouble myself about what it will or will not hold, or what in the future will be mine to have or to have not. Today is here for me to treasure. I have the precious moment at hand to love and to cherish—the eternal now to give me joy. For the first time I truly understand these words: "They that sow in tears shall reap in joy."

With tears drying on my cheeks I drive the remaining miles over the slippery streets and slip safely back into the snow-banked driveway. The car is toasty warm and cozy now. The children are chattering. Their presence and the car's heater warm me, and I am wrapped in love for them. The light left on in the living room shines through the thin, white lace curtain, welcoming us and calling us in. We are alone but we are warm and filled with the peace of Christmas. Mr. and Mrs B. have been Santa and Mrs. Santa to our spirits, and I have been given three precious and fragile gifts—the gift of friendship, the gift of tears, the gift of now. These gifts and my children are mine to treasure and to nurture. Feeling part of the miracle that is Christmas, I am now ready to prepare a place for the birth of the baby in the manger of my own heart. And I know that the moment now will always be with me—mine to unwrap and to live. Each moment is a nativity.

– *Carol C. Ordal*

For Claire

I watch your small face in December dusk
as you wait for candlelight
and your chance to parrot the blessing,
and remember your great-grandmother,
the stories of her you will want to hear,
which ones to save,
and where one would begin.

One could begin with candlesticks:
that night before my wedding
when she presented me
with the tall silver pair
(regulation bridal-registry elegance)
then held forth
on proper Sabbath display.

Then, tongue softening,
she took me to the kitchen
and from the string and screwdriver-drawer
pulled out those small pale pewter sticks,
hardly five inches tall—
pocked, dull, munition-grey, caked
with old wax.

She talked of leaving Vienna
for Rotterdam in 1939,
in the back of a moving van
hiding among feather comforters
with the cranky baby
who would eat only chocolate.
Her mother had sent her off
with those leaden sticks
and she promised to light them—
each Sabbath, in steerage and after—
and remember.

I took them that night not knowing
one day I'd be saving them for you—
you, whose name, and hers,
means "clear, bright, shining,"
your laughing face
smeared with chocolate,
your wild hair flying
backlit by candlefire.

– *Elizabeth Stoessl*

The Loss

This section on loss is the most luxurious in the anthology.
These women allowed themselves the time to face their loss, to
grow from it, and to write about it.

Women have oh, so many roles in this life—Mother, Sister,
Grandmother, Aunt, Lover, Wife, Teacher, Cook, Healer, Activist,
Career Person, well, the list goes on and on. Sometimes we
don't grow until we are faced with a loss. No matter what our
particular 'abandoned shell' is, often the first step in the process
toward healing is one that most men can't relate to: giving
ourselves permission. Permission to grieve, to hurt, to heal, to
scream, to say no, to walk away. Allowing ourselves the luxury
of focusing on our selves, our pain, our growth, our celebration.

Sometimes at night, I reach out half asleep
Expecting without knowing it
To touch his solid warmth
To know that even in sleep
He will turn and gather me close.

from *Sometimes at Night*
by Jean Carpenter

ellen alone

at sunset she watched the slicing forearms pumping as if they were
attached to wheels, cutting gold ravines in the water.

when there was no comfort in strength, she found herself noticing
small things: the sound of crows walking down the roof,
the horsefly's blue-green wings.

accepting the inevitable narrowing, she had chosen. she had decided
on her gamble, and the rest of infinity trailed away from her
in the dark water.

still she has her doubts.
was it wrong to drown her sacrifice in coffee,
to paint large, sheltering trees in the hallway?

she can say that she has no regrets, but what will she trade
her life for? she can have almost anything now:
start again, minus twenty years—go.

she is twice the swimmer's age, she estimates, that boy
glistening and hers, rising out of the ocean into a photograph,

who left his silk underpants with an inscription for her to find
just yesterday, cleaning out the bureau.

a garden. a small plot. time to paint, and sing without anyone
telling her to stop. some days she could drive out to the mountains

and speak her mind. but still the mines he planted there. please, a
small fertile place on the edge of the lake where she can turn the soil
with her hands and not uncover *your man forever, love, j.*

–Jacqueline Marni Olkin

the air between us

everything holy is happening
suddenly at this table
so often it happens at tables
in the aftermath of a good meal
amid the debris, bread crumbs
and wine spilled on linen

no linen, no wine today
in the ambulatory care cafeteria
spills cover the tan formica
a tweed hat covers your scalp
we spent half and hour walking
up here from radiology

the air between us is thick
your coffee spoon is heavy
just months ago you promised me
lunch at a fine hotel
not what we thought would happen
this fearsome holiness

I always used to be asking
and now your life is a question
a question addressed to me
and leaning across the table
leave whenever you're ready
and then I will have you always

– a.c. fowler

Bedside Spring

We gathered in disarray
and raucous joy
at seeing your gamin face—
the twinkling eye and mischievous grin—
framed in white against
the hospital bed.
Your grip pressed blessing into each hand.
Vivaldi and Tchaikovsky evoked
the cycles of the years
and the seasons of our lives.
Breaking bread
and drinking wine,
we were content to be with you,
to be with one another,
to be.

That night,
we glimpsed
the sacred
in a tree.
We drank
the gold of God
and learned
to love dandelions.

– Sheila Gorg

journal entry

I give too much of myself away.
I love you too strongly, I'm there for you too often,
    in too many ways.
You've already told me you don't want it,
    always pushing well-intended gestures aside.
I try too hard. I'm too excessive.
Want to be everything, do everything, want to have
    everything figured out.
Giving other people too much of my attention and energy and focus.
Too much on you and not enough on me.
Don't want to have to explain myself to you, give away myself to you,
    to care for you, not me.
For I don't look after myself, I look after you.
And that is a mistake, and how I have become disappointed.
I appointed myself in you. But I am not you.
And you have only wanted me when you want me.
I'm not going to try in such a way that depletes me anymore.
I'm feeling used and it's half my fault.

– *Lisa Miles*

Reveille at Fort Worden

(At the Conference)

I wake up rough, sinuses
squeezed against my eyes and the bed sheet
slipped off the corners like nobody's friend.
Everything hurts from the flat army bed
fastened to the wall at both ends. My neck
hurts, the spine running down my continent
to the hills—my right hip hurts, and my knee
is its usual dome of pain, augmented by fog
lifting through the pines.
Birds are fully at it—their bright clear optimism
soaring tree to tree. I sit on the bed considering
Homo Erectus, wonder if I still classify,
and in any case, how will I get to the bathroom
and resurrection.
Where is the girl who graced the playing fields
in every sport, who leapt into sloops
and pulled their strings like marionettes, or hiked
the high country of the Tuolumne? She lives
in lush memory.
Where is the girl who said *never,* refused
to hold hands with weight, closed her joints
against arthritis, rejected the call of age.
She's curled inside, annoyed as hell, but in the end
as she will this morning, she's the one
who unfurls, and forces the pulleys
and levers to action. She sends messages
to muscles and tendons, reminds ligaments
of their job descriptions, insist on vertical
and finally, over an indignant period of time—
hoo-ray, up she rises.

– *CB Follett*

A Celebration for Ginny

you spent the first
half of your life
rejecting God
the second
trying to make contact

atheism
is a form of religion
you said
never taking God
for granted

expecting to be reborn
at whatever time
in whatever place
on whatever terms
you had earned

with no inclination
for surgery
radiology
or chemotherapy
you nursed your silent pain

until silence
became the statement
that death is unimportant
because energy
never dies

old girl
I see you dancing
in your next life
as a leaf in the wind
as a dervish.

–Joanne Seltzer

Requiem for a Womb

As in a tintype, I stand on the primordial beach
With dark, looming trees reaching from the lakeshore
   To the gray sky.
Like a seeker, I steep myself in the warm comfort
   Of one misty pool after another.
But none offers the embrace of that rich, fruitful ocean
   That released me so long ago.

– Sheila Gorg

passage

ben walked past the pictures
in the hallway without noticing,
but they were following him with their eyes
to the last door, ellen's room.
he sat lightly on the bed,
afraid to speak.
the room was dim with one amber lamp,
and the rust colored walls and the persian rug
were somber and imploring, and the plants leaned close.
'mom," he said in a tone surprised at itself;
ellen sat down beside him and narrowed her eyes,
"do i have to be the man of the house now?"
but the words broke up after 'man' and
she took his shaggy head in her lap and cried
for them both.
the room kept a respectful distance,
but watched intently, protectively
over its charges.

−Jacqueline Marni Olkin

Aunt Rose is Dead

I looked around my office. My desk had grown into its usual organized mess. Soon my secretary would remind me that my desk should be cleaned by quitting time on Friday. She had told me that every Thursday since the second week I joined the staff. Her high pitched voice and superior tone never changed. Blue file folders had been placed neatly on the corner of the mess—Franklin, Gerber, Hill, Irons, Jensen, Katz. That the files were F through K made me think, "F—K, how appropriate."

The orange numbers on the digital desk clock given to me by co-workers for my 50th birthday told me I had one hour and forty minutes to quitting time. I still had to tell the head nurse in the Williamsburg wing what Mr. Madison's lawyer said about the lawsuit, go to the Richmond wing to make sure enough aides were scheduled for the weekend and talk to Mrs. Peterson about her lost laundry. I knew Mrs. Carney would catch me somewhere to remind me that nothing was being done about keeping the UFO from landing on the roof, waking her between 3 and 4 p.m.

After work, I would go to my apartment, feed the bird, have a Lean Cuisine, followed by Ben and Jerry's Cookies and Cream, watch the news, Wheel, and Jeopardy. Sometimes this routine could be varied by checking my clothes for the morning before taking a shower and going to bed with "New Procedures for Patients with Parkinsons," an exciting new publication from the Virginia Board of Nursing Homes. What a life!

I swiveled my chair to stare at the courtyard. The day's rain had knocked the petals off the last of the pink and yellow roses and made the white mums muddy. Pretty soon someone would be out there planting those purple cabbage plants that make me think of my Uncle Hank's midwest farm. Uncle Hank's farm, I mused, picturing the golden, glittering wheat fields and was about to hum a John Denver song when I saw Mr. Russo enter the courtyard from a door that is supposed to be locked. He liked to romp naked in the wet grass. He had just begun to unbutton his trousers when I called an attendant to help him back into his clothes and room. "Will I ever try that, too?" I wondered. "Probably, next month if this mood continues."

The five-minute drive to my apartment took fifteen minutes because the roads were wet. When I got into my apartment the light on my answering machine was blinking. The message was from my sister... "Hi. Aunt Rose died in Florida. She'll be buried in Indiana on Monday. It's your turn. Call me. Carl has all the details."

"But perhaps the funeral is the answer to an unspoken prayer. ..."

"Aunt Rose was a very nice lady," I said to my bird Randolf. "But perhaps the funeral is the answer to an unspoken prayer. I can go back to my roots for a long weekend to be with the wholesome, sane people of my childhood. I will get away from the craziness and the crazies at West Fairfax Seniors."

I fed the bird and gave him a new seed treat string before making three phone calls. The first one went to my sister to let her know I would be able to get away. After our parents died, we began taking turns going to the funerals of aunts and uncles. Secondly, I called United to make reservations. Staying a Saturday night and going for a funeral made for a reasonable ticket price. Lastly, to Carl, an older cousin, who used to take me for rides on the International Harvester and push me into the sky on the tractor tire swing. He promised a familiar face would greet me at O'Hare Airport on Saturday afternoon.

Work went quickly on Friday even though my mind seemed to be filled with images of Aunt Rose. She always wore a cotton dress, covered by an apron, white anklets and black wedgies. She was such a gentle soul. The last time I saw her she was just the same. My desk was clean before noon. There were no unmanageable surprises. Actually, by 4:00 p.m. I found time to finish a letter to relatives of residents that wouldn't have to be mailed for a week.

Saturday was the kind of fall day that reminds me of going to college football games. It was everything a fall day should be—clear, sunny skies and an occasional crisp breeze. On the descent into O'Hare airport the gray and black ribbons of highway with the match-box cars looked like any other big city's traffic, but the deep red of the maples and the taxi-yellow of the oaks let me know I was in home territory.

As I went through the gate, Carol, Carl's younger sister, greeted me with a smile and loud, "I would have known you anywhere."

"Good thing," I thought, "You don't look like anyone I know." I never liked Carol. As a child, she was always bugging Carl and me. Probably, I had dismissed her from my memory. Maybe I didn't expect anyone dressed as she was. She wore a neon-green skin-tight jumpsuit, red-sequined sneakers, and a purple cowboy hat draped with an orange nylon neck scarf. Actually, she looked a lot like Randolf. The colors looked better on a lorikeet. I don't know if people stared at us because of her loud voice or her costume.

Following the signs, we made it through the maze to pick up my bag. Finding the car was like trying to find an informed salesperson at a discount store. We tried four different lots. Carol's giggles became louder each time we had to re-enter an elevator to return to our starting point. I would have preferred being with a group of crying preschoolers.

Once in the car, I relaxed for a time while Carol dug into her studded saddle bag purse for the parking ticket.

Within minutes we were going south to Indiana on the Tri-State expressway—a practice track for eighteen-wheeler drivers who plan on entering the Grand Prix. At that point I realized I should have made a stop at the ladies' room. Carol was unabashed as she wove through Allied Moving trucks, Exxon tanker trucks, and whatever else she could pass. My eyes were shut when she said, "Don't be afraid. The trucks are my friends. I was a logging truck in my last life." I did open my eyes to see her face before cautiously replying, "I didn't know one could be an inanimate object in a previous life."

"According to an in-depth article I read in *Horoscopes, Yesterday, Today and Tomorrow,* you can. Of course, I knew I had been a truck long before I read the article. You know, it's just something you feel."

"Oh," seemed the only response. I then asked if we could stop at an oasis (a rest area) to use a rest room.

She happily agreed. Seeing an oasis ahead she crossed three lanes of trucks in seconds to reach the exit, unaware of the protesting horns and screeching brakes. I took my time at the rest area. Too bad alcohol is not sold there. I was able to find a Sominex in my purse that I hoped would work as a tranquilizer. Back on the road, I asked her more about her present life. She had six cats, one dog, four white mice, and twenty-two fish, all friends from past lives. The previous week she had seen a seven foot python that was an old friend but didn't have the money to buy it. I was very happy that I had decided to stay in a Best Western.

Dropping me off, she said, "I have to feed the gang, but I'll be happy to stop by to take you out for pizza later."

"Gee, thanks, but I've made plans to see a high school friend tonight. I'll see you tomorrow afternoon at the funeral home. Thanks for picking me up." I wanted to call out, "Keep on trucking," but checked myself.

I called Joanne. She would be there in an hour. After a quick shower, I was feeling great. I went to the lobby to wait.

While I recognized Joanne almost immediately, I didn't remember her being so attractive. She wore a cream-colored sweater, blouse, slacks, and shoes. Her short brown-blonde hair was softly brushed away from her face. Her green eyes sparkled and she smiled broadly as she quickly strode toward me. Right then, the six year old tan blazer covering the forty pounds I had gained since high school made me feel old and dowdy.

We went to "Graceland." What had been a place for burgers and fries thirty years ago had been transformed into an upscale full-fledged restaurant. I ordered a Bud. She ordered a Manhattan straight up.

"I was so happy to hear from you," she said, sincerely, I think. "What marvelous things are you doing with your life? You were the one with the brains to go to college. Did you ever marry or were you too smart?"

"I'm a director of a nursing home. It's interesting and challenging but I may be ready for a change. No. I never married. You've married several times. Think you'll try it again?"

"If I fall in love and he's rich," she laughed.

Over salad, we reminisced about the great times we had in high school as seniors. During the main course, we exchanged gossip about classmates. Joanne said she had planned on calling some of the old gang to let them know I would be in town but just didn't have the time. Eating our raspberry sorbet, she told me about the great men in her life and, how wonderful her sex life had been since she was 45. I didn't tell her my last date was when I was 45. By the time our cappuccino came, we had exhausted our conversation.

I was back at Best Western in time to watch the 10:00 p.m. news. I decided it was good to be in bed early in order to be at my best when I met the relatives. I wanted to fully appreciate my roots, my grounding.

Eating Sunday breakfast at McDonalds, I overheard the conversation of the two women at the next table. Both women wore jeans and beaded sweatshirts. One had long orange-red hair pulled back with a navy bow. The other one had jet black hair cut into a modified crew cut. Red had a mouthful of pancakes as she said, "I just knew that Joe would leave Sam to return to Leslie."

Even though I was sure I didn't know the people, heck I didn't even know who was male or female in the triangle, I listened more intently.

Blackie struggled a tad as she picked up her egg McMuffin with three-inch red nails accented with silver glitter and continued, "I figured Leslie would forget about Val since the mugging. Ya know, he's been comatose for weeks."

Red took a sip of her orange juice and sighed, "At least Eve's (Yves?) heart transplant has been successful, so now wedding plans can continue."

"Good thing, the baby is due soon,"

"Isn't it amazing how they all just go on, in spite of set-backs and real tragedy?" said Red, shaking her head in empathy. "Of

course my husband thinks I'm weird getting so involved in a
TV show."

"Husbands, can't live with them. Can't live without them."
Blackie said sagely.

I thought a slight detour in my return walk to the motel,
passing my elementary school, would be fun. As I walked down
Arizona Avenue, the houses looked a lot smaller than they did
when I was a kid. Some people had enclosed their porches.
Some had built garages. The tree branches now touched each
other across the street. Small amounts of dead leaves had
begun to gather near the curbs. Curbs...I wondered when those
got put in. I turned left at 63rd Street. I got to the middle of
the block. The two-story gray clapboard St. Andrew's Elementary School had been replaced by a six story semi-circular
brick St. Andrew's Hospital. After staring awhile, I trudged back
to my room.

Virgil, the funeral director, greeted me at the funeral home
that afternoon. My parents and his were friends. Virgil, his
brother, Jake, and I used to play Monopoly in the apartment
above the funeral home while our parents played pinochle.
One summer night Virgil, five years older than Jake and I,
convinced us it would be helpful if we filled the ambulance and
hearse gas tanks with water from the hose. He had also locked
us in the coffin room more than once.

Virgil smiled his most sincere smile as he said, "You
haven't changed a bit. I would have recognized you anywhere.
How have you stayed so young while we have all aged?"

Suddenly I realized why I have never trusted funeral
directors. I said, "Thanks. Pure living, I guess. Is Jake here?"

Virgil's smile vanished and he spoke in a whisper. "Jake left
the business. The family was really disappointed. Dad never got
over it."

"What is Jake doing?"
"He is in medicine, geriatric research. One of his sons helps me
out on weekends. So there is hope."

"Let him know I asked about him. I think I'll see my
relatives now."

I didn't remember so many windows in the Father O'Brien room. Maybe it was the brightness of the day. No, the room was much darker when my father died eight years before. The heavy maroon velvet drapes had been replaced with white sheers and shutters. The now green tweed rows of padded folding chairs to the right of the double doors used to be black. My mom used to borrow them for parties. I wondered how many times they had been replaced since my high school graduation. The now pastel striped walls were lined with soft, comfortable looking large-flowered sofas and love seats. Instead of the usual bank of flowers around the coffin, some containers of flowers were scattered around the room, smaller ones on small natural wood stands.

Unfamiliar people sat quietly, staring at the front of the room. A tall distinguished looking gentleman came toward me. "Anna, it is so good to see you. So wonderful of you to travel so far. Mom would be happy."

"Carl," I responded, as I gave him a hug. "How are you doing? How is your dad taking it?"

"Okay. Let's go talk to him."

Uncle Hank still looked as mean as ever. His voice, however, was smooth and kind as he said, "Anna, she always had a special place in her heart for you. She loved your Christmas cards with updates on your life. You gave us lots of chuckles over the years."

"I'm glad I could be here."

Muddled thoughts distracted the prayer I said at the coffin. I blinked away the tears and felt sad mainly because of the years that had passed without seeing her. Rose was my favorite. Rose always seemed to have the time to listen. Sometimes I would take the bus to her farm on Saturdays. Mom and Dad would pick me up Sunday afternoon before visiting Grandma. When I got old enough to ride my bike, I often biked both ways. Every summer I would spend a couple weeks on the farm. She heard complaints about my brothers and sisters. When I was in high school, she dried many a tear over a low test score or unrequited love. When my parents just couldn't understand, Aunt Rose at least pretended she did. She would hug me and tell me I'd be fine. She didn't give advice.

After a few hours of trying to remember names of faces that the years had changed, Carl invited me out for a hamburger. He seemed to be the same kind, patient person I remembered teaching me chess and bridge. The years had treated him well. His blue pin-striped shirt with a white button down collar enhanced his handsome face. He was Mr. Conservative. Half-way through our quick dinner, I felt comfortable enough to ask, "What happened between Betsy and you? I always liked her."

Carl hesitated a moment before saying, "Another man."

"It's hard to believe that Betsy would even look for another man. You're really a nice person."

"Betsy was not the one with the other man."

Several seconds elapsed before I recovered and said, "Do you still have a relationship with this same person?" The word "man" would not come out.

"He'll be there tonight."

Many different people were at the evening calling hours. Uncle Iggy, not an uncle, and his real name was Stanley, asked, "Why'd you let yourself get old? You shoulda got married." He philosophized through a toothless mouth.

Alice, his wife, elbowed his ribs and said, "Anna, remember those words come from an old man with gravy on his tie and pee on his fly."

Aunts Sophie, Marie, and Evelyn were huddled close to the coffin arguing softly over a recipe for chlodnik—a beet soup I hated as a child and still refused to eat. Carl's daughter was unsuccessful at keeping her seven year-old twin boys from pulling petals off bouquets and putting them down unsuspecting callers' backs. Carl's lover, as good-looking as Carl, politely went from mourner to mourner always saying the appropriate thing. The few teenagers there looked especially uncomfortable during the praying of the rosary.

Aunt Julie (age 87) left early, complaining of her rheumatism, but confided to me that she wanted to "watch that hunk, Kevin Costner" that night. I refused the invitation to go out for a drink with Carl and friend. I did, however, accept their offer of a ride back to the motel. I was suddenly not sure of the safe streets of my childhood.

Looking at myself in the mirror the next morning, I wished I had not stayed up to the end of *Dances with Wolves.* Oh, well, maybe people would think that my eyes were bloodshot from crying about Aunt Rose. Another glorious fall day greeted me as I went to breakfast. I wondered whose car I would be in for the ride to the cemetery. After my grandmother's funeral twenty years before, Aunt Rose didn't speak to Aunt Sophie for months because she was in the third car instead of the second car after the hearse.

I was not surprised with the new Our Lady of Sorrows building. I had heard some people talking about it the previous night. I was surprised, however, that there was no mass. A woman, not even a nun, conducted a scripture service. She even gave a short sermon. I forced myself to listen to her. She talked about the difficulty of living each day, accepting our lives, and adjusting to change. I watched Uncle Iggy try to stay awake. I watched the twins try unsuccessfully to be quiet and not bother each other. Carl and Uncle Hank sat in the front pew, their tear-brimmed eyes glued to the statue of Our Lady of Sorrows for which Aunt Rose had organized the fund-raising. I rode in the fifth car to the cemetery. After the burial Carol asked if I wanted to walk to my parents graves before driving to the airport. Nodding yes, I started to walk slowly through the fallen leaves.

Grabbing my hand, Carol said to me, "I read that it is safer to walk through a cemetery holding hands."

I began to kick the reddish-brown leaves as I took her hand. "Carol," I said, "I thought I was headed in the right direction but I don't see the right graves. Do you think they moved them?"

"They're a little farther down...There...See, you're in the right place. You just didn't know it."

On Tuesday morning, Mr. Madison met me at the nursing home entrance. He met me most mornings, demanding to go home. "Oh, come on Mr. Madison," I said gently. "This is home. You know you like it here."

– *Salome Harasty*

Marilyn: An Epilogue

We said goodbye today.
In winter's own coldness,
            we stood there in the silence
            and wept;
Not for the suffering she had endured,
            or the pain,
but for ourselves;
who had lost the wisdom, comfort, happiness and friendship
that this one being had put into
            our lives.
It was all so trite in the end.
      The announcement,
      the weeping,
      the viewing,
      the final gathering.
In a few days we came to accept the passing
      of one soul we'd taken a lifetime to understand.
And then, like gossips,
      we competed among ourselves;
      not allowing one to remember more than another.
Our own consciousness pondering what we could have done to
keep her here longer.
The tree stands one branch lighter today;
      its nakedness whistling a sad song.
All it can do now is stand and remember
            the seedlings that must grow alone,
                  and rise out of the soil that gave them life;
                  where they began and will eventually return.
The stark reality frightens those who are left.
It is not that we are afraid of death;
            or the finality of life.
                  We rather choose to forget.
But mortal spirits don't exist
      and in each soul that departs
      we admit the immediacy of our own end.
So we cry,
      and pray,
            and remember,
                  why today we said goodbye.

                                          – D.E. Irons

115

Slow Learner

I have learned, but slowly, about
the unrelenting absoluteness of death.
You'll note I do not say finality;
My schooling is not finished.

When I was 15, my grandfather's death was a ripple
That barely disturbed the placid surface
Of my awareness. But I never forgot the feel of it.
    Cold
           unyielding
                  packed earth.

A few years later it was an aunt, gone before
her time, no older than my mother. I began to be
aware of life's uncertainty. Death's choices were
    unaccountable
           illogical
                  random.

When it was my own father who was suddenly
gone with no warning, it was a violation of
My sense of immortality. I was
    shocked
           affronted
                  outraged.

My mother-in-law had boundless energy,
love of life and beauty, devotion to her family.
But all that strong life force wasted away
    hopelessly
           slowly
                  painfully.

A gaping hole was left in all our lives.
Death was implacable, insatiable
A hungry deity that demanded the
    strongest
        brightest
            best-loved

Each time, the sacrifice is harder, the
demand cuts deeper. I should know by now,
be ready. But once again it has caught me by
    surprise
        alone
            remembering

Opportunities not taken, moments not shared,
feelings not spoken, comfort not given,
pleasures not offered,
    selfishness
        sorrow
            regret.

I would curse and cry out at the unfairness.
But that would be like cursing clouds
because they drift across the sun
    Death isn't fair
        or unfair
            it simply is.

I no longer worry much about whether
it's an end or a beginning, because I know
that whichever way it turns out, nothing
        I believe
            nothing I do
                will change it.

–Jean Carpenter

Weather

in memory,
the Reverend Richard Martin

On Sunday, the doors
to the Spaulding Rehabilitation Center
freeze open. Snow whips through the lobby.
The elevators don't come.
In Room 703 you are whispering
mysteries, ruined fragments
of prayer you once knew by heart.
But then, clear, telegraphic,
from that other country—
can you forgive me? On Tuesday
no spark, only the low
captive moan, the aimless thrashing
under your restraint. On Thursday
snow begins at noon. I kneel
beside the bed, boots dripping
onto the linoleum, lips pressed
against your ear, insistent.

I have to shovel out the Datsun.
It plows through mounting
drifts, past vehicles abandoned
on every incline. A mile
from home I leave the car
in the Middle School yard, climb
the Common Street hill. Inside
I take my first swallow of whiskey
stare out the blank window.
It will always belong to you
January, storm, this mix
of death and weather.

– a.c. fowler

Healing Hands

It was a warm day in late summer when we made the two-hour drive to the veteran's hospital in the mountains of West Virginia. The gentle breeze stirred flashes of gold and green in the poplar trees, revealing the results of a dry summer.

The hospital was set apart from the city, located on a hill overlooking farms on one side with the city spreading across the Piedmont plane between the knoll and nearby mountains. We wound around the spiral drive, encircling the flat, angular building with its numerous jutting wings, each an external duplicate of the one before, finally reaching the visitors parking area in the back lot. The hospital seemed remote by design, as if to further remove the inhabitants from the mainstream of life—setting them apart bodily, as their illnesses distinguished them physically from the rest of the vigorous world.

My parents and I had come to visit my father's nephew, a veteran of World War II and the Korean conflict. After suffering bouts of illness over the years, he had collapsed with liver disease. Most of his 50-plus years of life had been tediously average and unsuccessful, spending his post-military career as a skid trucker in a local paper mill. Characteristic of his lack of direction, he had served first in the Army and then in the Navy in hopes of finding the key to his purpose in life. When that failed, he turned to alcohol, much as his father had done a generation before, as an avenue of escape from the meaninglessness of his life.

I did not know my cousin well and had not seen him since my childhood. Our family was not in the habit of reunions; we gathered occasionally for weddings, but often for funerals. His crisis came during my brief home visit from a teaching position overseas. I was grateful for the chance to see him, even under these circumstances. Somehow, the family ties felt vitally important to me that day.

After negotiating the inner mazes of corridors pungent with the smells of illness and sterile antiseptics, all identical with beige tiles and cream colored walls, we finally found Bob tucked away in a private room. The pale green room was small, barely accommodating the hospital bed, a straight-backed aluminum chair, and a narrow bedside table. The shades were pulled to filter the afternoon sunlight. A single mounted shelf loomed over the spare metal nightstand to the right of the bed on which were three get-well cards and a bowl of cold, half-eaten soup. Bob was lying on his side in a semi-fetal position under the sheet, looking surprisingly small even on a single-size bed. The top of the bed was raised to support his upper body, and the cold metallic rails were in place to prevent him from falling—or from escaping, I thought.

"I reached for Bob's bony, outstretched hand and was amazed at the strength of his grasp."

Never a robust man, he now weighed 95 pounds, with yellow-tinted skin stretched over frail bones. Bob's eyes were dull, focused on some blank spot on the wall. His hair, once a rich dark brown, looked dry and straw-like, threaded with streaks of gray. His liver had sustained much damage from years of alcohol and neglected diet and his body finally had reached the limits of revival.

His wife Ruby was there, tired and drawn, but making an effort to be cheerful. She led us out into the hall where she could speak confidentially. "It was so good of you to come!" she said. "We have received your cards and flowers. But, you know, he's too weak to hold the cards. I must hold them up and read them to him."

My father and I reentered Bob's room, while Ruby slipped away for a quick lunch in the hospital cafeteria. My mother joined her to keep her company. "Where are you staying? she asked. "Who drove you to Martinsburg?" Ruby's replies were lost in the distance of the corridor as they continued toward the other end of the hospital.

We stood tentatively beside Bob's bed, my father doing most of the talking. "Remember when I used to take you and Jim to Sunday School? You must have been all of twelve years-old then," my father remarked. Bob smiled. "You always took an interest in our schooling. And I always appreciated your visits to mother when her cancer was so bad," he continued. And the conversation drifted into memories and reminiscences of Bob's youth and family events. Bob became more animated during the twenty-minute visit, but when one of the nurses cautioned us not to tire him, we decided to take our leave. Bob was obviously moved by our visit. He reached for my father's hand, shaking it with more vigor than we thought he possessed.

Ruby and my mother returned. My mother patted Bob's hand, assuring him that we would visit again soon. I reached for Bob's bony, outstretched hand and was amazed at the strength of his grasp. He held tightly to my hand with an energy that surprised me; he must have held on for some thirty seconds or more. I was reluctant to pull away, sensing that some energy was passing from me into Bob, although I felt no change in myself, no loss of vitality. In fact, I was a little disappointed not to "feel" a tingle, a flow of energy—a tangible indication that something unique was occurring.

As I walked with my parents through the parking lot, I shared my wonder at the handshake.

"We must come back next Sunday," I urged. "We cannot wait two weeks. He might not be with us that long."

The following week we made the pilgrimage back to the veteran's hospital, only to find that Bob's private room was empty, the bed neatly made and all signs of occupancy missing. For a few minutes, we feared the worst. Then a nurse saw our confusion and directed us to his new location on the ward. He was sitting up playing solitaire. "He's like a new man," the nurse said. "I've never seen such a come-back with a case like his. It's really remarkable!" We marveled at his apparent return of health. Even though he was not completely well, his color was nearly normal, his eyes were brighter, his life-force visibly restored.

I was intrigued by the miracle before us. But I could not explain what had occurred during the first visit. We spent more time with Bob, enjoying his company as he obviously did ours. As before, my father did much of the talking, this time with contributions from my mother. I listened, but said very little. Bob seemed to draw energy from our presence. There was hope and expectation in his words, enthusiasm in plans of returning home.

At the close of our visit, the ritual of handshaking is repeated. Again, Bob held tightly to my hand as if to connect to the flow of a life force. I remained within his grasp, clasping his hand as he did mine until he released me, not wanting to sever his connection to whatever source of energy we had tapped. Yet, I could not question Bob as to the long, firm handshake, or what he felt from them. It might have broken the spell.

"Again, Bob held tightly to my hand as if to connect to the flow of a life force."

By now, I had magically associated Bob's progress with our visits. Somehow, his return to health was linked to us, and we could not neglect him. I encouraged my parents to return with me the following Sunday. We sought him in the ward, but once again, we were greeted with an empty bed. Puzzled, we asked at the nurse's station. "Oh, he was so much better that he checked out this morning and left with his wife," the nurse explained. Perhaps our visits had turned the tide for him.

* * *

It was more than fourteen months later when I saw Bob again. He was back in the veteran's hospital on the same ward and in his original room. This time, he was dying. His illness had again manifested due to a resumption of his drinking, only with more severe results. He had returned home to the sameness, the ordinariness that had spawned his drinking. With nothing to alter the pattern, and no awareness to tap into a source of life-giving energy, Bob had resumed the insidious, destructive lifestyle that had put him in the hospital the previous year.

We stood mutely at his bed side, listening to his labored breathing that was costing him such effort that it was his main focus. His eyes indicated that he knew we were there, but his body could do little to acknowledge us. His yellowed skin was transparent now, barely shielding the thin veins and prominent bones. Life-sustaining tubes were connected to what little tissue remained. My father patted him gently on the arm, said a prayer for him, and assured Bob that we were there for him. Much as I wanted to do the same, I now feared the magic of the earlier visits. I dreaded to touch him and risk pulling him back into a life that would probably repeat this final chapter of suffering for him. We remained a few moments longer and then left in silence.

– *Neva A. Clayton*

On the Same Winter Night That Claire DeFosse of Spencer, Massachusetts, Was Shot and Killed By Her Husband, Ernest

I send a prayer for the doe
with her red leg tonight in the woods
done with running
resting there now in the cold
lying in the white sheet of moonlight
the blood drying
her furred flank sighing
breath into life
and out

I send a prayer of thanks
for the full moon she holds
in her round brown eye
a prayer for surrender
of the fur and the breath
a prayer to mark
this deer life
and death

– Connie Hershey

Marie's Prayer

These are words that Marie might whisper
to us if we would listen.

Dearest Family and Friends,

When you grieve, mourn for yourselves and for one another. But rejoice with me, for at last I have come home to take my place at the banquet that my Father prepared for me before I was born. Know that the sunset of my life with you is the dawn of a glorious and unending life of unimaginable peace and joy.

All the saints were assembled to welcome me: my mother, whom I have missed so; my father, eager to embrace me; and my three babies—more fully human and fully alive than if I had given birth to them.

When you think of me, remember the times that the world would call inconsequential: long nights of aimless chitchat, hands clasped carelessly as we ambled along the beach, girl talk over afternoon coffee, and dodging one another as we worked about the kitchen. Remember the laughter that produced tears and the giggles that took our breath away, and especially the silliness—that absurd mirth of intimacy and memory.

I am waiting for you here, but you need not hurry. Time means nothing to me now. Whenever you come, I am here. And until then, I shall be with you in the gentle, cooling breeze; in the cleansing dew; in the soft glow of dusk; and in the first burst of sunrise.

I was ready to return to my Father. What more can I ask of Life than freely and hopefully to embrace Death?

God bless you; I pray for you, and I wait for you.

– Sheila Gorg

Tea Roses

Ben is on the sidelawn
    in the damp grass under the birches
        gripping an imaginary golf club.
On the stone wall stands
    his glass of gin and bitters.
He swings again and again
    at an unseen ball
        aiming it over the meadow
aiming at perfect form
    his slim hands clasping
        the cool evening air.

Around the corner in the cutting garden
    John Larsen is weeding, staking
        foxglove and gladioli.
His blunt fingers coax
    and marshal beauty. Always
        he has managed my mother's flowers
and now he comes to me
    on Sunday afternoons. But he may
        not touch the roses, they are my own.

Across the field, church bells
    begin to sound for Evensong.
Across the field in the church yard
    little Ben is buried, my son.
I think of roses, how they grow
    the roots of rosebushes,
        underground, and I long to be
with them all, underground.

On the sidelawn Ben practices:
    address position, full body coil,
        pivot, right side release.
John Larsen takes his wheelbarrow
    toward the toolshed. Tendrils
        of fog lie on the bay.

– a.c. fowler

Faith in Time

My knee caps were beginning to pain from this kneeling position, but I knew it would only be another few minutes until Father Daniel finished giving the eulogy and we would all go home and be done with it. The service had passed fast, actually, maybe because I had stopped listening about ten minutes into it, and instead began remembering a life that seemed so long ago to me now. I leaned closer to the casket and folded my hands on the shiny brass bar that jutted out almost half way up the rich cherry wood casing. It was a beautiful coffin and I could not help but think that Harold didn't deserve something so nice, but his daughter wouldn't have it any other way. My thoughts drifted again. I studied my hands and the tiny roof strands of veins that ran from my knuckles to my wrists, and tried to recall each and every time I had daydreamed about this moment: staring down at my lifeless husband and feeling no remorse.

> *"LeeAnn made up her face for as long as I could remember, and Peggy used language that made the man who delivered the oil for the heater look up and display a blush."*

I met Harold Ives on my eighteenth birthday. I was staying with my grandmother for the summer in Norfolk, Virginia, along with my older cousins LeeAnn and Peggy who were fourteen months apart in age. LeeAnn and Peggy took me to the Wander Inn, a local bar to celebrate my arrival as an adult. I remember the night well because it upset my Oma (a name given in affection to my Irish grandmother by my German father) to know I was going out with my cousins. As much as I knew she loved all of us very much, I knew I had a special place in her heart. After all, I was the daughter of her daughter, a daughter who's only disappointment to her was that she had not outlived her. My cousins on the other hand were the daughters of a son she no longer knew, and begot by a woman for which she had no liking. "Untamed," she called LeeAnn and Peggy. "Good girls at heart, but untamed." I smiled whenever she whispered it to me. It was our little secret, because I knew exactly what she meant. LeeAnn made up her face for as long as I could remember, and Peggy used language that made the man who delivered the oil for the heater look up and display a blush.

Beginning about the time I was ten years old, I would spend a month of my summer in Virginia. LeeAnn and Peggy spent most of their time hanging around the store on the corner with a bunch of the local boys, throwing rocks at trees and pooling money to buy soggy ice cream sandwiches from Otto's freezer at the service station.

Being three years younger than my "grown up" cousins, I wasn't invited along on those summer afternoons. Instead, I spent my days with Oma eating ice pops on the old sofa on the front porch, and watching game shows on the living room television through the window screen. Oma walked around the yard pulling weeds from her flower beds and yelling occasionally to neighbors about the heat.

On the night we went to the Wander Inn, Oma was in a foul frame of mind. She walked about the house complaining about her bills, and that the roof was in need of repair and where was she to get the money to pay for it.

Oma had cooked a special dinner for me: turkey, mashed potatoes, gravy, and cranberry sauce. On Thanksgiving, I hated it, but in June it was the only meal that I thought would be special. LeeAnn and Peggy rushed through their meals in order to get ready to go out. They had neglected to tell Oma what we were planning to do until the instant she questioned why everyone was hurrying so. She looked at me disappointed, "Laurel, do you really want to go to that place?" she asked.

"She was on the porch in the dark, sipping Coca-cola through a straw stuck in the neck of the shapely green glass bottle."

While Peggy and LeeAnn were upstairs arguing about who was going to wear the red and white polka dot halter top with the matching drop earrings, I went downstairs to speak to Oma.

She was on the porch in the dark, sipping Coca-Cola through a straw stuck in the neck of the shapely green glass bottle.

"Oma," I said, "Please don't be upset about us going out tonight. We'll be careful. I promise, I'll try to get them to come home early." Oma was a heavy set woman in her late sixties, with short reddish brown hair beginning to streak gray at her temples. She had a scarred complexion that nobody ever mentioned. She had long since stopped farming the land and had managed to keep the house after Grandpa died by renting two small cottages at the far end of the property. She rented one of the cottages to a Negro family, which had caused a great stir throughout the town. Eventually, the others realized that the Wrights were good people as Oma had known from the start. All quieted down.

"Laurel, I have never worried about those two upstairs. I gave up on them when they were about half as old as you are now. I knew there was never anything I could do to help them. They had different blood, the blood of another woman I knew nothing about. How could I help what I didn't know about," she said distressed, almost defensively. "But you, I know about. Your mother, she came from me and I knew what things went on in her mind, and soon will in yours. Because somehow it all works out the same unless you really try hard to change it. I just wish for you that life would be different, a little better than what me and your mother had. Do you understand what I'm trying to tell you? Mistakes made early in life never go away, whether you want to believe it now or not."

I wasn't expecting this kind of talk to come from Oma, I really didn't think she thought that deeply about her life, or mine. I heard the racket from LeeAnn and Peggy's shoes clanking down the hardwood stairs. In no time they would be out on the porch.

"I understand Oma," I pressed my lips into the smooth fatness of her cheeks. She just picked up her soda bottle and continued to gaze across the lawn.

The Wander Inn was lit from every corner to the next with small blue and white lights competing only against the constant parade of headlights from the cars pulling in and out of the parking lot.

Inside the Wander Inn, the dim light couldn't quite make it through the clouds of smoke that hung in the air. I followed my cousins as they pranced proudly past the pool table and up to the bar, stopping to wink or whisper "hello" to men they recognized.

"This is my cousin, Laurel," Peggy announced to the barmaid, a woman in her late forties who was trying to cover it up with too much make up and cleavage. "She turned eighteen today. We're here to celebrate. Give her an Old Granddad and Coke." I was thankful for her experience in this situation. Harold Ives was sitting at the bar to Peggy's right and must have heard every word she said because when the barmaid brought the drink back I found myself drinking a toast to my birthday with a man I didn't know.

Three weeks after I'd met Harold in the Wander Inn, I was packing my powder blue vinyl cardboard suitcase and moving out of Oma's house to jump in a coffee-cup littered, cigarette-stinking truck to travel the Interstate to South Carolina with him. Oma called me a "fool girl" and said "I'd never listened to a thing she had tried to tell me." She waved her hand in the air and informed me that I was breaking my Daddy's heart, and hers as well. But what did Oma know about me and my feelings, and about Harold and our feelings, or for that matter, how the presence of a man in a woman's life can transform all?

It was exhausting in the beginning, but I endured. I went from never missing a shower in the morning to having to wait for nearly three days before I could bathe. The first couple of months we were together, Harold made stops all the time so we could clean up and sleep for a while. It didn't matter much where we stopped, any place was just as good as the next as long as there was a bed in the room and a liquor store and deli close by.

Later on, Harold hated to stop along the way, and said it caused us to lose too much ground. We ate quickly in the cab, and I slept curled up with my head on the armrest most nights, unless Harold was in the mood for some "fun." And even then we only stopped for a few hours, usually at the kind of place that had movies in the room. Since it was usually days since I had a good night's sleep in a real bed, I would fall asleep the minute my head hit the pillow. Harold would watch the naked people on the scratchy television screen while he breathed hard and churned on top of me.

"His big burly presence reminded me again of the ugly in my life that the soft, needing little person at my breast had helped me to forget."

Sometimes I'd protest. If I was very tired, or hurting, this was when we started to fight. Nearly a year after my eighteenth birthday, I was again searching for freedom.

On a trip to pick up a load of grapefruits in Florida, I asked Harold if we could stop to visit a friend that lived with her grandparents in a retirement community. He agreed to drop me off for the afternoon and said he would come back to pick me up at eleven-thirty that evening.

I waited with Jenna until 3:00 in the morning at the gates outside the complex (the truck was too big and noisy to fit through the little streets of the miniature community). Harold never showed. At 3:30 Jenna left to go home, begging me to come back with her. I waited until the sun came up, dosing on and off, leaning against a brick pillar. Finally, Harold drove up at 7:00, smelling like he did when we spent the night having "fun" together. I didn't say a word to him for nearly two hours, until I asked to stop at a gas station because I felt sick.

My Regina was born prematurely seven months later on a bitter cold January morning. Harold was driving a load of plastic bottles to a Coca-Cola bottling plant in New Jersey. He made it back to see her before she turned a week old. I'd been living in a furnished efficiency in a motel just outside of Arlington since I was four months pregnant. Harold decided I would be better off staying at home than on the road with him. I was sad when Harold walked through the door. His big burly presence reminded me again of the ugly in my life that the soft, needing little person at my breast had helped me to forget.

Regina was walking now. Harold came and went, always taking something somewhere. I gave up caring and trying to figure out how long it should really take him to make the trip, or if he would come home to me. I put the pain of my unfaithful husband out of my mind and went frequently to the free clinic to get checked. I was always so embarrassed. After I'd been there for the third time in four months, the doctor took me into his office and asked me if I thought I needed counseling. "'Cause a woman just doesn't sleep with so many men like this if nothing is wrong," he said. I started crying and told him about Harold and he said he was sorry to have assumed, but that I should still think about talking with someone because living a life like this isn't normal either. This was the second time I considered life without Harold.

It was nearing the time when Harold was due home from a haul when Peggy called to tell me that Oma had a stroke while working out in the yard that afternoon. It wasn't until two in the morning that Mr. Wright noticed there were no lights on in her house and came over to see if something was wrong. "She'd been lying there dead in the weeds probably all day. The mail man feels terrible, says he probably walked right past her when he was there at 2 o'clock," she said in a casual tone. In my mind, I went back to my summer days spent with Oma, long before Harold, I could see her tugging weeds from the ground and stuffing them into the pockets of her apron, delicate strands of roots and dirt dangling as she walked. I left a note for Harold telling him what happened and that I had taken the bus to Norfolk with Regina and would call him when I got there.

When the bus reached the station, I was happy to get off. Regina had been cranky and fussed more than half the way. I recognized Peggy pacing about on the platform. She appeared tall and slim, much the way I remembered her to look, only with a few mature additions. She came running toward me but stopped just short of throwing her arms around me, as though a voice had whispered in her ear at the last second to stop. I reached for her affectionately and it felt as though I had hugged a statue. The uncomfortable coldness caused me to back up. I looked into her eyes for an explanation. She looked down at Regina hiding between my legs. My child was so shy.

She did not know many people. She didn't even know her own father from a stranger.

"I'm sorry I called you," she said. "You really didn't need to come all this way."

I was confused. How could I not come? I loved Oma just like everyone else did. Did she expect me to get back on the next bus and go home without even paying my respects? Didn't my father want to see his granddaughter?

Her face was stressed. "Laurel, you can't tell anyone I'm the one who called you. I only thought you should know. I didn't expect you to come all this way with the...," she looked down at Regina again with a blank look and continued, "baby and everything."

I reached behind me and grabbed Regina, contorting to pull her up into my arms. Once up, she immediately wrapped her arms around my neck and buried her face to escape being seen.

"Are you telling me that I'm not wanted here? Is that what you're saying?" My voice was high and girlish. I could see a hint of guilt in her expression, but not enough to reassure me that I wasn't all alone in this world now. All alone except for my timid child who had begun to whimper and tug at my hair.

"It's not that," Peggy stumbled on her words. I noticed Oma's emerald and silver filigree engagement ring on her finger.

"You made Oma very unhappy, with what you done, running off with Harold, and the baby and all."

I held Regina tighter, in my own way telling her that her existence was not wrong. She began to cry harder and louder, squeezing my neck tighter. Intuition told me she would hang on long enough for me to break my grip with one hand and bend down to pick up the suitcase from the floor. "Hang on sweetheart," I whispered, kissing her sticky wet cheek.

I walked away furiously, unaware of where I was going. Regina and I sobbed in unison walking out to the row of hissing busses waiting in the dimly lit lot, their doors opening to swallow up the people as they walked by.

"Why didn't you come for me?" I asked Harold as I walked in the apartment door. Suddenly, I expected something of him.

He didn't answer because he was sleeping off the empty bottle of whiskey on the dresser. "I called you over two hours ago and you said you were leaving right away to pick us up at the station!" I yelled at him. The room smelled of urine and I noticed the dark spot on the carpet in the corner of the room.

I gently let Regina slip from my arms onto the sofa, her small puckered lips parted slightly, but her rhythmic breathing never altered. I moved the coffee table in front of the sofa and tucked a blanket in the space in between to keep her from falling. I was suddenly saddened at the thought that my child had never slept in a crib of her own.

I stood in the half darkness, looking across the worn carpet and smelling the sickening scents within the room. I was startled by Harold prying off his boots with the ball of his foot. The first boot hit the floor causing Regina to exhale a little louder. The second boot hit the first, canceling out the sound. I was sickened to look at him, smell him, or think about the way I'd been with him. Then the thought that he was a crucial part of my existence and more importantly, Regina's, silently erased the disgusting thoughts.

The pain in my knees had progressed into a dull numbness. I will be embarrassed to be the only one standing so close to the grave. Regina leans over, puts her arm around my shoulder, and whispers into my ear, "Momma, if your knees hurt, go ahead and stand. People will understand." Anything she tells me I know is right. Just like her spirit. Everything is right. She stands nearly five feet seven inches tall, with her height coming from her father's side, and she has wide set brown eyes and curly sable hair that comes from me. She's made another life for herself, a life different and apart from mine, a life that would have finally made Oma proud of our female line. I never doubted her quality or strength. I gave her all I had to give. And the rest she produced naturally, from within.

— Marie A. Sylvester

Sometimes at Night

What I miss most are the quiet moments—
not necessarily the talking
or the shared experiences, not even the
shared memories, not moments when I crave
to reach out for someone who will
know that I only want a hug
a moment's closeness.

Sometimes at night, I reach out half asleep
Expecting without knowing it
To touch his solid warmth
To know that even in sleep
He will turn and gather me close.

Once I dreamt his arm across me
Felt its weight
Touched its shape and the texture of the hair.
As I broke the surface between
Asleep and awake, I knew it couldn't be him
But the sensations had been so real
I was astonished to find myself alone.

–Jean Carpenter

Hospital Room

Unnatural loveliness with grey-not-pink
Blushes on the morning's opalescense;
You lie in sheets. Machine lights bleep and blink.
Hours drop through I.V.s in slip-dances.

All round, the room grows gradually bright,
Day's boundless largess filters through fresh panes,
Noon hits the face—sleep grows big with night,
Down a narrow hole you drip—pulse wanes.

As you drift off, I sit and also doze
—Lights spin into erratic flights of flies.
Together we turn into midnight flows
—Block the growing sun that other souls eye.

Although we may not always stay one eye,
We're bound so close that both our noons now die.

– Joyce Cook

The Place

In the high moonlit room you lie
sleeping next to me, your right hand
still clasping my left breast.

Outside, bare branches of oak,
catalpa, creak in the night breeze.
Your hand, your arm, rise and fall

with my slow breath. I imagine
the fields behind the old houses
—your mother's, your grandmother's—

remember how you've said,
I want to go back, to lie down,
to hold the place in my arms

again. Your fingers close.
In your dream do you see
our world, a second world

for you to rise from the grass
and love? Outside, the full moon gleams,
pulls at the tides of the Earth.

– a.c. fowler

Are You Happy?

Old friends.
We truly are old friends.
But we know so little of each other's lives.
What's her child's name?
How did he get to be 12? Wasn't he just born?

We really should write more often.
But our letters are stilted, superficial.
What's his name got an A on his report card.
Doctor husband went to a medical conference.
I travel a lot.

I play our early days like a favorite song.
It repeats the intimacy, the sharing, the searching
Of girls discovering the meaning of life,
Dancing en pointe in leotards
and playing tennis

She always won those games and made A's in school.
But there was a melancholy overriding the victories.
A quiet holding back. I never could quite fathom it.
Yet we shared something important—
I'm sure of it

Shy. We were both shy and quiet.
Much alike but worlds apart.
The melancholy pervades her presence even now.
"Are you happy?" I ask at a brief holiday visit.
"Sometimes," she says.

Dreams never took her where she wanted.
She never quite smiles. She never quite laughs.
Write to me, I ask her. Send me an e-mail.
What would I say, she asks.
I don't know, she answers herself.

The envelope comes. Inside is paper lace and pink paper.
Went to New York for a large dose of ballet, she writes.
Husband had a conference there.
But are you happy?
Yes, she lies.

– Cynthia C. Rosso

137

The Self

Because of their struggles and losses, the women in this section write of learning to trust their own voices and talents. They write of the Self and the struggle to maintain their sacred identity within the confines of society.

> *I am a strange child to myself. A strange child*
> *with a sickness that will not get better.*
> *If I adopt myself to love and protect,*
> *I may lose myself after a while,*
> *After the manner of all things*
> *that eventually die.*
>
> *Or, I am like a beautiful woman to myself.*
> *I want me, yet do not feel worthy*
> *to have such a woman fall asleep*
> *and wake again with me.*
> *And even if she did, could I give*
> *her solid love?*

from *The Beginning of January*
by Mary Diane Hausman

Stacking Wood

The morning after "Orin's Firewood and Taxidermy" delivered two full truck loads of wood cut to twelve-inch lengths, seasoned and split, I pulled back the curtains in my bedroom window and saw the enormity of what I'd done. Twin mountains of logs looked like they'd fed on yeast cakes overnight and risen to fill the available space. The skirts of one pile fanned across most of the side lawn, its companion cascaded over the front yard and the parking area, and both seemed a full story high. The night before, darkness had swallowed at least half of my order as it was dumped there, but by crisp October daylight, three generous cords of wood coalesced into one monumental stacking chore.

"So strong was my sense of unity with the environment that I lost track of time, surprised, when I thought to look at my watch, that two hours had passed."

The house that needed this impressive supply of fuel for the wood stove—in addition to a full tank of oil, mind you—sat mere inches from the ocean, surrounded by Casco Bay in Maine, on an island just big enough for one other house and barely connected to a more substantial point of land by a bowl of sand and rock that flooded with every high tide. Harsh coastal weather systems and the island's exposure to the elements often combined to blow open locked doors, set off smoke alarms, shoot torrential rains through cracks in the thresholds, and send me to bed mighty early with a "Walk Man" blaring Mozart in my ears to blot out the thunderous roar of the wind and the thrashing of the sea.

I was a tenderfoot in that corner of the universe. I'd arrived the month before to spend a year writing, and did so every morning, but in the afternoons, although my legs twitched with the need to get exercise, I'd shrink from thoughts of going out for a walk. Even on a good day, when skies remained mostly blue and low tide rolled around in time to clear out the causeway linking me to the mainland, steady winds of twenty miles an hour or more coming across the cold Atlantic kept me huddled up inside, thinking mainly of my fragility. "Wait until the temperature goes up, until the sun stays out, until the winds die down," I told myself time and again, still unaware that those three conditions would never happen simultaneously in that place. Then the wood arrived, making it plain that I'd better be prepared to work outdoors every day or the logs on the bottom of those piles would freeze to the ground in their disarray while the rest would be covered in snow.

I put on layers of sweaters the first couple of days and wore a pained expression, "Poor me. Cold and alone on an island, having to fend for myself." I looked at my watch every few minutes, hoping at least an hour had passed so I could pat myself on the back and retreat indoors for a cup of hot tea. But as the rough outlines of my wood pile began to emerge, my body started responding to the activity as if it addressed some primitive physiological need I'd been neglecting since childhood.

The excessive layers of protection I'd once assumed against the teeth of the wind lay shucked across the yard one by one, thrown off in the heat of labor. Sweet, cleansing, plentiful sweat trickled down my scalp, soaked the collar of my turtleneck, and banded the waist of my jeans. Cheeks aflame, muscles supple, I bent and hoisted armloads of wood to the rhythm of waves upon the rocks and songs of the feasting waterfowl. Muddy paths veined the yard as I repeatedly retraced my steps from the chaotic jumble of logs to the squared-off ends and lined-up rows in my masterpiece of a wood pile.

I inhaled the aroma of earth, wood, and water. Rather than closing down to resist the anticipated assault of coldness on my skin, millions of pores seemed to open themselves wide, drinking up the moisture, the daylight and the underlying vibrancy of the natural world. Porous, I developed a sense of molecular connection to the universe: I was the air that it breathed and it was the air that I breathed—all in one, in and out. So strong was my sense of unity with the environment that I lost track of time, surprised, when I thought to look at my watch, that two hours had passed.

I worked in billowing fog, in flurries and in drizzle, making beautiful stacks of wood as high as my shoulders and as long as the skiffs drifting by on the bay. Sometimes as night or a chilling rain began to fall, just like a child, I would protest, "I don't want to go inside!" The wrench was nearly physical, a ripping of the fabric of the universe torn ragged in the spot where my presence had been. When I returned from my year in the wild, people asked if I thought the experience had changed me. "Yes," I said. "I'm tougher now."

– Susan D. Anderson

Knowing

Knowing goes twice as far as knowledge,
It goes down twice as deep
for it comes up from within.
Knowledge is the spark that lights the knowing
for it's already changing me.
But knowing is a flame that grows.
It's both soft and strong, cool and hot.
A courageous me, no longer afraid of my own fire,
sits with knowing.

– Susan Galbraith

Lord, in My Heart

for Countee Cullen

Holy haloes
    Ring me round

Spirit waves on
    Spirit sound

Meshach and
    Abednego

Golden chariot
    Swinging low

I recite them
    in my sleep

Jordan's cold
    and briny deep

Bible lessons
    Sunday school

Bow before the
    Golden Rule

Now I wonder
    If I tried

Could I turn my
    cheek aside

Marvelling with
    afterthought

Let the blow fall
    saying naught

Of my true Christ-
    like control

And the nature
    of my soul

Would I strike with
    rage divine

Till the culprit
    fell supine

Hit out broad all
    fury red

Till my foes are
    fallen dead

Teachers of my
    early youth

Taught forgiveness
    stressed the truth

Here then is my
    Christian lack:

If I'm struck then
    I'll strike back.

– *Maya Angelou*

The Beginning of January

December passed without cry or laughter.
There were blissful times. Many.
A full month in a space of my own making.
A full month spent with myself.
Now, the snows of January fall.
A white softness, sometimes treacherous,
wraps itself around the house and neighborhood.

I am spellbound by my own hypocrisy.
Taken in by the whiteness of my words
the blackness of my actions.
It is not necessary, this calculated planning
of work that will not be done.
It is not done because I myself hold the small key
that will open all for me.
And I do not turn the key.
I only talk as if I will.

When am I not thinking forward?
When am I not thinking backward?
It is a riddle I do not try too hard to unravel.
The pain from a year ago is gone.
The pain of recognizing that I am a statistic.
The one in four girl-children taken
By men, who eat when they are not hungry.
Men who seem to not know their appetites
make no sense.

My memories have been tempered by growth and time
and new love deepening like the root
of a tulip bulb planted in late fall,
just before the ground has become too cold
to accept it into her skin.
The love grows slowly, tentatively,
afraid it too will die before its time,
Will be left for a bigger something or
someone more beautiful.

Still, I learn that solid love makes room
for pain and doubt. And though
I know myself less and less,

it seems, I have more and more.
All my life I have had nothing and everything.

This is the truth:
(It is hard for me to accept)
I do not need. I only want.
And in the wanting, I think I need more than ever.

I am a strange child to myself. A strange child
with a sickness that will not get better.
If I adopt myself to love and protect,
I may lose myself after a while,
After the manner of all things
that eventually die.

Or, I am like a beautiful woman to myself.
I want me, yet do not feel worthy
to have such a woman fall asleep
and wake again with me.
And even if she did, could I give
her solid love?

This is the truth:
(It is hard for me to accept)
I am a sick child. I am a beautiful woman.
And, I am strong enough to love both.
Am strong enough to be both.

I walk to the window, shaded by a black mini-blind,
Lighted by the white of snow outside
I wrap my arms about me,
hold them steady against my breast
Then drop them to my sides.
In this gesture, I turn the key,
release the lock.

Through the opening
I see that I am solid and white and black
And being such, I am everything
and I am nothing. I accept this.
Now, I can laugh.

– Mary Diane Hausman

The Dream of the Somnambulist

"If you understand Truth, why have a teacher?
When the disease is cured, why call a doctor?
After the water is crossed, what use is a boatman?
To a man without passions, what use is a sorcerer?

—*Nagarjuna, an ancient Indian sage*

In struggling to find clarity, as I wander in a vast network of dreams, an image is awakened—a shadow by a window who is always peering out with her head against the glass—pressed so close that her breath continually fogs the pane so that the view on the other side seems forever blurred and hazy.

I have this recurring dream of the somnambulist—looking for windows in her sleep, seeking ways of opening these windows, and struggling to find a passage to the other side, to escape outside herself, into another form or maybe to become a mere force—to exist without existing, to influence the course of life without being seen, without form, without identity.

To perhaps exist as the sweet rain or as the gentle hint of wind.

To one who has wandered many epochs in the shadow world, not quite considered a full being in her own right, as women throughout millennia have experienced, to be on solid ground all too often is to see life as a cage and oneself as a frightened bird—fluttering nervously without purpose behind bars—always looking out at freedom, but instinctively knowing that it is better to resign oneself to the cage until the day finally comes...

So the somnambulist floats along, yet with passion, with the frenzied anxiousness you often find in dreams, down streets and paths and in an interesting maze with distracting, yet peculiar diversions, being allowed to enter a kaleidoscope, full of interesting, colorful designs, but always turning, turning, endlessly in the same circle of familiar patterns.

"Illusion works impenetrable,
Weaving webs innumerable
Her gay pictures never fail,
Crowds each on other,
veil on veil."

Emerson's words, not her own. Yet she struggles to hear her *own* voice in the sleep walking. She can only hear the voices of the masters—so many she has read, knowing she will never be among them, at least not in this incarnation. She trips over piles and piles of books in this labyrinthine dream, always has a quote for every occasion, but cannot feel completely proud of her own utterances, or her own visions...yet all the talent in the feminine voice, only now being recognized on its own merits and not just as an adjunct to the traditional male canon of literary, musical, and artistic genius...Yet she still often looks to others to conjure illusions through losing herself in love.

"Yet she still often looks to others to conjure illusions through losing herself in love."

So, half incarnate, half spirit, she pushes onward, mistaking eros for caritas, the profane for the divine, desire that lasts for an instant for love that is everlasting, continually falling into the same snares like a rabbit caught by more cunning predators. And she knows the trap exists, yet she enjoys the chase, the thought that perhaps in time she will elude all, even herself, or that perhaps magic can turn the wolf into a lamb, a friend.

The trance walk continues...The magus waves his wand, pulling flowers out of hats, convincing her once more that the illusion is real—only this time the illusion is much stronger, for reasons unknown to her. Perhaps, she has cast a spell on herself. She returns to her room and is suddenly awakened. She stands next to her bed and then sits on its edge. Two candles burn.

Try to stare into the flames of both—you can't
Your attention gets diverted from one to the other
The impossibility is disheartening, like trying to
stare into another's eyes—you can only seem to focus
on one completely

149

And in the end, both flames will be extinguished
the eyes will lose their power to hypnotize and
the fire will burn all the way to the end of the
wick without you having captured the magic of even
one flame—trying too hard to consume both with a
single glance, like trying to walk on two separate
paths at the same time

How can Janus face himself in the mirror?

In the night, during dream time, our Janus faces are forced to look at one another, and all the polarities merge, sometimes painfully, as we awaken to our true selves. Yet, also during dream time, we can escape the earthly bonds that keep us immanent, tied to our roles, which hardly ever bespeak our essence. The path of this somnambulist is to discover a way to keep the morning light from obscuring the fantastic vision of dream time.

– Dawn Chamberlain

Mask Portrait

Your face is like a mask.
It peels off in the quiet night,
which smells of orchids and ink
and reflects in the candlelit mirror
along with your face. Nightbird cries
as you feel your untouched skin
and taste the salt from uncried tears.
The sorrow on your tongue
is an ancient rock of fear.
Perhaps the same rock that Sappho
tossed into the Aegean
thousand of years ago.
But, she did not throw rocks.
Yes, you wear your mask daily
painted with red and blue and pink and beige,
colors not of the flesh.
You are not a yuppy, even
though you are small and pretentious
and your computer is off-line again.
As the velvet blue screen of brainwaves
shocks your body daily,
you sink to greet it.
You fly to Jupiter,
but only on the weekends.
Little Mollie is in there, somewhere,
one day to rise and greet the world
in barefeet and scrubbed-clean face
to tell stories and play with words
using colored pencils to dig in the earth.
Que sera sera
the pencils say and then weep
as you tediously apply your
morning mask.

– Mollie Cox Bryan

With Myself

She moves me,
moves my mouth for me.
This inner voice,
this incessant, chattering nag.

Tonight she makes
the stillness come alive
with judgement and criticisms
and all manner of self-effacing,
outward facing
tarnished jewels of doubt.

I cannot look her in the eye
I cannot read her lips.
All I can do is stand
here in the dark
before the forest,
stars dropping sparkles
above my head,
and listen to her sharp tongue
as I catch words flying
across my ears:

"Why didn't you explain yourself clearly?"
"Why didn't you say this?"
"Why didn't you say that?"
"Why didn't you stay quiet?"

I walk the circle of
the four directions:
East, to bring the vision
South, to trust it
West,
Ah, West of Death and Rebirth:

help let my critic die
and I will give her
a proper burial.

Just as I ask
North for white light understanding,
two bats fly above my head,
fly into the west.
The West of Death.
release the struggle within myself
to their black-winged silence.

It appears the critic is gone.

Before the night is done,
Owl cries at my window.
And knowing that the dying
sometimes struggle a bit
before their final release,
Critic, her voice my own, answers Owl:

I am not done yet.

– Mary Diane Hausman

Labor of Dreams

There are babies seething inside me
Writhing to get out.
They may just rip my skin
to get free.

It does hurt this constant birthing
Of things I cannot hold for long.
Some die before their first cry.
It's my own fault—
I suffocate them under my tongue
Or beneath my heavy fingers that refuse
To lift a pen or brush or chisel.

The ones that make it
Well, they fear dying, too!
So are persistent in their pushing.
Till at last I give up,
Ignoring their sucking mouth and
Squinting eyes and grabby little fingers
I take a deep breath,
Open my legs, and let them slip
Or pour or jump or carve
Their way out and push up my breasts,
Squeeze my nipples till the milk runs red
And I feed those hungry little souls
Till they fall asleep across my eyes,
My chest, my belly.

I lay back on the pillow of my
Efforts, gaze at my little babes
Of every color and texture across my canvas,
Every word spread across my desk:

Green and Sky
River, Mountains, and Tear,
Push and Shove,
And slide down into
Sweat and Bone, Pearl
and Flashy White Smile,
Poppy Blood
And Oozing mud.

Then, I think,
Yes, these are the
Ones that wanted to be,
To be here bad enough to hurt me.

And all the hair-pulling and sobbing,
All the ignoring and making-love
Instead of, going-to-pieces,
All walks for days on end and
Long drafts of a cold one,
All the sitting and staring out the window
Make no difference now.
These babies were meant to come.

These dream babies,
These brush strokes of my thighs, these
Penned wisps of my eyelids flutter.
These precise cuts of my carving tool fingers.
They were meant to come.
I couldn't stop them. I tried.

It's a good thing they didn't care
What I wanted.

– Mary Diane Hausman

Glastonbury

One moment I am walking
The sidewalks of a busy market town.
The next I have stepped through
A gateway in the stone wall to tread
On ancient earth, thickly carpeted in green,
Among the abbey's crumbling walls.

The noise of traffic and commercial bustle grows
muffled, distant, a faint echo from the past—
No—from the future?—I cannot tell.
The spirits of the Old Ones press close
Around me. Surely, in all this crowd,
There is someone who knows that I am here.

Eyes closed, my spirit reaches out, groping
In the stillness to touch another seeker.

– Jean Carpenter

The Seeker

Kneel them down praying, butt to knee, all the robed men
who led her through life. They'd reach to Mecca

or at least to Lourdes. First was the blond-bearded Christ
who gazed down from the Sunday-School walls, and his henchman

who handed out blue Christmas sacks filled with ribbon candies
and one chocolate drop, after he told the story of The Miracle Birth

but he wouldn't tell her what the word "Virgin" meant, so
she couldn't figure out what the miracle was all about.

At eight, her friend the pastor's son prayed for a bicycle while his father
listened. He got it. She prayed only to God and got no bike that year.

At thirteen, she promised her soul in secret to Bishop Sheen, whose
    eyes burned
through the twelve-inch Zenith as he pronounced her guilty, thrilling
    her so,

rescuing her from the pale Calvinist at the Sunday pulpit who
    dispense crystal
vials of Welch's Presbyterian blood and tiny squares of Wonder Bread.

Later she became a Jew. She did it for love—for the sad-eyed Rabbi as well
as the one for whom she forfeited her heritage, hymns and all.

The Maharishi sniffed roses and giggled while he peddled secret
    mantras. Just in case,
she bought one. When she divulged it, she learned it was not unique.

After the Buddhist retreat, it all became clear: simply to follow the precepts
of the brown-robed one—live in the moment, follow the breath, do not
    fear death...

Now at a certain age, she is through with all of them. She contains all
that she needs...but next week, the Dalai Lama is coming to town...

– *Elizabeth Stoessl*

Flexibility

"Tractable: the capability of yielding, responding or conforming to changing or new situations." Webster's New Collegiate Dictionary

Before dawn, I rise in the stillness of the night, in the quiet of nothingness like a neverending dream. I drink my favorite herbal tea and reflect on images that pleasantly haunt me as I stretch and genuflect to my soul and to the universe. Still in my pajamas I reach for each wall, the unattainable ceiling, my toes, as though I am greeting the four directions: East, West, North, and South while I stand centered in the process of readying myself for the day.

After twenty minutes of yoga I sit down and write a poem or a part of a story, (sometimes vice versa), revise what I've already done or continue, knowing that I am flexible enough to change what yesterday seemed composed in stone. So it is with my life. I am not rigid; I am able to bend in tune with the force of the wind or weather, yet strong enough not to break. We must all meet our challenges and traumas this way. We need to be able to think and act quickly at various times in the day or in our lives to stave off anxiety and panic that would destroy an unsuspecting victim, who, if unprepared, gives in to defeat, failure, illness, obstacles, tragedy. The mind is related to the body and vice versa.

Flexibility is possible at any age and has everything to do with our surviving the vicissitudes inherent to modern life.

– Rochelle Lynn Holt

The Well

'The Well' was a woman's cross-disciplinary creative collective that met regularly in Pittsburgh, Pennsylvania from 1991-1994. Its members were Lauren Judith Krizner, Tina Gelfand, Lisa Miles, Catherine Singstad, Susan Spier and founder Adrienne Wehr. Together, their talents included painting, acting, music, filmmaking, movement theatre, writing and sculpting. Now the waters of 'The Well' flow anew, having re-grouped in 1996, reaching out to include even more women.

We are constantly 'performing' as we live and cope in this world because we are masking our hidden sides and our sometimes crippling features. In 'The Well' we examine that which forces us to so perform throughout life. We are unmasked. Women who have formed, certainly with struggle, our own identity. Now resources to each other.

In 'The Well' we are performers, artists and creative individuals who have stepped away from the venues we know best, to explore the irony of our other 'performances.' We find ourselves moving, using music, ritual, being still together, and always discussing those topics of intense mystification to us. In the journey inward, we've pondered performing to others' liking, and now contemplate performing to our own. This, from an original goal of gathering to create a specific cross-disciplinary piece.

We have worn masks and rejected them. Just in communicating with each other, things are demystified. Just our collaboration unmasks us. Though we are indeed using our talents, the vehicles through which we best express ourselves, we aren't performing in 'The Well.' We are ourselves—our creative abilities finally presenting themselves in their most unique voice, echoing the genuine selves that we are presenting to each other.

Linda Schierse Leonard, author of *The Wounded Woman*, speaks of attempting to express the female experience via "art forms through which we can be in the mystery of that experience and yet somehow articulate it too." It is in this very shadowy, powerful way that we honor our feminine nature in 'The Well.' With the intent that we will only perhaps share our collaborative work with the public, we're confident that our meetings bring each of us individual strength.

– *Lisa Miles*

Appeal to a Higher Authority

we are the citizens of the commonwealth
converging in strung out lines
baseball caps turned backwards
revoked licenses in our pockets
leaning against dirty yellowed walls
in the Registry of Motor Vehicles
sitting slouched on slatted benches
waiting for our numbers to come up

we squirm before the Board of Appeals
as parts of our bodies grumble
not-quite-polite requests for lunch
we face the grayed face of the clock
the slow etching of the blue minute hand
our eyes rise to the ceiling a maze
of bared ducts and wires and hanging
flourecent lights suspended there
speakers rigged dangling from the pipes
crooning Begin the Benguine

outside the second story window
jackhammers crack into spring
we cannot see the perfect cloud
pausing over the detoured traffic

show us
another way
to transport our selves

– Connie Hershey

Discovery

There is a fountain
inside me:
all I need to do
is listen
and the music
will flow.

– *Lois Ames*

Stillness in the Storm

The tree sways in the wind
Wild storm whips its' branches
Red and yellow leaves descend
dancing across the field.

The core of the tree is still.

The ocean swells into waves
Wild storm stirs its surface
Foaming surf pounds the shore
leaving tidepools in its wake.

The depth of the ocean is still.

The grass bends in the breeze
Wild storm flattens its blades
Field shimmers light and dark
revealing the path of the wind.

The roots of the grass are still.

Where do you hold your consciousness?
Just on the transient surface?
Whipped by every wind,
victim of every storm?
Settle into your core,
plumb your depths,
sense your roots.

At center you are still.

– Stephanie Noble

Writer's Blocks

My husband doesn't seem
to like my writing much.
Last night he locked the
Reveal Code key up.

No question with my dad,
who asks how much is paid on
publication—he'll pay
more, if I keep quiet.

Each new poem, my sons
swear, show the world
which of them I love best—
always the other brother.

Still I can't let them
deter me. My poems are
where I find them to be
more than mere
men.

– Pam Stolpman

The Weight of Things

I
This attachment
to things and their curves,
to soft colors and
mild alliteration,
deeds in wood and lace,
does it paint me
fragile—
rice paper stretched
on a painted fan?
Does it separate me
from the brown leaves
lying in the woods,
reshuffling themselves
with each wind?

II
The wind shifts around the corner
of my beautiful, armored house,
heavy with its silver radiators.
Little breaths escape
from under blankets here
where my children sleep;
toes stretch
outside the covers.
Too warm,
we say,
it is too warm.

I think of tiny dried fish
glittering in the Chinese market.
I feel no moisture,
no mistakes.
There is a river
to carry me, no puddle
of impetuous little lives
splashing the lace,
not even one magnifying drop.

I turn paper,
to shreds of parchment.
I lie in ash.
One puff of wind and I would
explode through the air, free
and attached
to no thing.

– Connie Hershey

The Path

You say perhaps this isn't your path
and I wonder how you can doubt
And then I say you are correct
this isn't my path:
it's a mighty river
I've stepped in
and I'm swept along
into white water.

You say perhaps you don't
have right reason
perhaps you seek this path:
to find a lover or community
and I wonder how you can doubt me
And then I say you are correct
this isn't my path
this is a waterfall
into which I've wandered
and now I am saturated
with rainbows.

You say perhaps this isn't your path
perhaps you should seek the path
of my sister
and I wonder
how you can misdirect me

But I say you are right
this isn't my path:
this is a dark, dry, dusty plain
and I, parched, am flooded
with a torrent of invisible rain.

You say perhaps this isn't your path
people aren't prepared
you are unripe, premature
and I wonder
how you can not know
that I'm already moving
like an arrow
let go from a bow
already set flying
seeking the Heart.

– *Lois Ames*

The Place I Ran To (Journal Entry)

I ran. Finally. I ran over to the path alongside the creek and kept on running. I thought my lungs would explode. That is what I wanted. I wanted my chest to explode. To open up and spew out whatever I've been keeping in me for the past week, month, year.

As I ran, I felt everything. I felt the muscles in my thighs contract beneath the jiggle of my skin; I felt my arms swing, my calves tighten and expand with each piston-like footfall.

> *"And as the bubbling white foam reached below the rock line and flowed out smooth, like glass, on down the stream, I knew I would find a calm inside my head."*

I ran until I couldn't run anymore. Mallards swam away as I ran over rocks like a mountain goat. I ran into the water. There, I found what I had come for—the water, rushing through and over rock, concrete, jams of leaves and sticks and rubble; the water, bubbling, like my brain.

That was it. "My brain is bubbling," I said to myself this morning before I went out. And now here it was. The bubbling water, like my brain, churning, gurgling nonstop. This is what I had run to see. I found a connection with the water. And as the bubbling white foam reached below the rock line and flowed out smooth, like glass, on down the stream, I knew I would find a calm inside my head. But first, I just needed to feel every piece of me in action. I needed to explode and hurt and ache and fly and feel everything.

I don't know if I can go one more night without making love. I need to explode like lightning; rip open a dark slice of the sky and feel my breath come in jagged gasps. Like when I run; when I make love; when I am touched deeply and to the core; when my roots are touched; almost painful, like Rinpoche's raw heart. Only when I am so exposed and raw and open do I feel real. Like the skinned horse in the Velveteen Rabbit.

That's why it's good to run. It's good to make love. You feel everything when you're so open and honest. You are real, even if for a moment. Until you take that last orgasmic breath then begin to breath evenly: in, out. Until that exploding flower, moments seem only an illusion. It has become a memory. A real memory.

There is an eternal "WHY?" that sounds off in my head every now and then. Now, more than ever, I feel this on-edge power; this edgy impatience, like the horse of the Dioscuri, Polydeusces and Castor, in Greek mythology. I chomp at the bit, my feet barely touching the ground. I titter. I tap. I dance back and forth, waiting to go somewhere but believing someone else must take the reigns and lead me. I feel like something is about to happen but I can't guess what. Perhaps it is simply my own "opening." My self opening, a petal at a time, while my center grows anxious to burst from the inside out.

I feel like Narcissus. Self-absorbed, learning about my own beauty, coming dangerously to self consumption, I tread the waters of aloneness that flow along the edge of togetherness. I'm never quite sure whether to keep trying to swim, or clamber out onto the bank, exhausted and awaiting rescue. My deepest fear is that no one will rescue me. In truth, I know no one can. But my fear remains; I will be alone and lonely.

My loneliness is a raven that flies across my left shoulder.

The raven is black and magic and tells me this loneliness is mine and I must practice it. Practice it so I may learn the difference between alone and lonely.

I can't quite see the raven. That is her magic. She is elusive. But when she comes I know it. I cry inside my heart. My heart weeps because I am finally beautiful and I am alone. Alone is my practice to be less lonely.

– Mary Diane Hausman

169

Contemplation

Where emotions wrestle and wreak havoc on calm composure,
To surface and recede in a troubling yet contenting tide—
Preparing us for who we are to become,
    (reminding us of who we are already)—
We are all fragments,
Shades of our soul like shards of glass
    that cut, yet reflect best, our presence.

– Lisa Miles

Spirituality

"Women's Spirituality" has become an over-used term. To some of us it means what it says. To others, it is the essence of the Self reclaiming its power. I wanted this anthology to hold the views and spiritual practices of a wide variety of women. While I myself may not subscribe to the same views of many of the women in this section, I can see the beauty in their practice—and the beauty is that it works for them.

While I tried to create a balanced book on spirituality, (my journalistic tendencies coming out in me), the anthology took on a spiritual life of its own. It pleased me that many of the women I heard from were questioning the 'patriarchal view' and the religious system which is built around this belief system.

For me, this section is the heart of the anthology—a sacred space that holds the words of the "Mother of Women's Spirituality," Z. Budapest, along with the prayers and meditations of the incredible women who contributed to this book. Add the strength and passion of Alice Walker's words and Rita Dove's precise eloquence, and you have a well-rounded section in scope and sphere.

Of all the places and spaces that women are still voiceless, spirituality is the most vital. It also is the place we most need to come together—dogma and labels aside.

> *Take me down, Grandmama God,*
> *under all my judgments of myself.*
> *Take me down, Grandmama God,*
> *under my bone weariness tonight.*
> *Take me down, Grandmama God,*
> *into the Earth, Your womb, Your cradle.*
> *Take me down Grandmama God*
> *into your warm arms.*
> *Hold me, Grandmama God, hold me.*

from *Take Me Down, Grandmama God*
by Mary Feagan

Initiation of the Shaman Drums

Invocation to the Fire Mother

Shamanism in my own country was the dominant pagan ministry. Both sexes could become shamans. This chant is one of the lessons taught shamans on the astral plane. The shaman would drum and chant under the full moon, beating her drum as her feelings dictated. From then on, the drum served as a direct line to her guardian spirits; whenever she played her drum, they would respond to her with help.

Blessings! Blessings! Blessings!
You are the white night's fire blessing!
You are the Queens's pure blessing!
You are my six-humped white Mare!
My six-eyed speckled tiger!
Thirty-headed Fire-Mother!
Forty-headed Virgin-Mother!
The cooker of raw things!
The thawer of frozen things!
The fanner of the green flame!
Robed in greed whooshing silks
She who descends on seven slopes
She who dances the seven dances
She who plays the seven games!
You are the Mother of the Triple Flame
Woven pearly horns upon your forehead!
You are the keeper of the stone hearths!
Thirty-headed Fire Mother!
Fifty-headed Virgin Mother!
Immaculate purity!
All wise scientist Mother!
Let our eyes see no evil
Let our hearts know no evil
Descend holding the white flame aloft
Descend encircling six times
Descend blowing forth blue flames
Be our Mother o whirl...
Be our Father o swirl...

Shaman Invocation to the Goddess of Spring

Upon my back my children sitting
pressing my back, protect me!
Upon my shoulders my children
Protecting my shoulders, protect me!
Before the Moon is full
At the sight of the Sun
At the beginning of the year
The fruit trees' blooming time
At the cry of the she-cuckoo
The Earth opens and green appears
The trees open and buds appear
I'll be there for you, don't fear!

– Z. Budapest
Holy Book of Women's Mysteries

The Great Charge

Hear ye the words of the Star Goddess
The dust of whose feet are the hosts of heaven
She whose body encircles the Universe:

I am the beauty of the green earth
And the white moon among the stars
And the mystery of the waters
And the desire of human hearts.

Call unto your soul, "Arise!" and come unto me
For I am the soul of nature
Who gives life to the Universe
From me all things proceed
And unto me all things must return.

Before my face, beloved of all
Let your divine innermost self be enfolded
In the rapture of the infinite.

Let my worship be in the heart that rejoices
For behold, all acts of pleasure are my rituals
And therefore let there be beauty and strength

Power and compassion, honor and pride
Mirth and reverence among you.

And you who think to seek for me
Know your seeking and yearning shall avail you not
Unless you know the Mystery:
That if that which you seek you find not within you,
You will never find it without.

For behold, I have been with you from the beginning
And I am that which is attained
At the end of desire.

– Z. Budapest
Holy Book of Women's Mysteries

Rose Window

Rose window at my feet, broken
A sliver of glass
held up to the light
glints without illumination
Fragile shards
scattered on the stone floor
—a jigsaw puzzle
I cannot solve
without losing fingers,
dripping blood,
forcing me to consider
the virtues of sacrifice.

Instead I find myself wondering:
Can broken glass be releaded
or must it be melted down and repoured?
Did I throw a stone through the window?
Is this really my puzzle to solve?

Then I notice a shaft of light
streaming through the arched wooden door.
It beckons.
Outside, there is a prism in my eyelashes
as the sun warms my skin.
There is a steeple in my fingers,
pointing the way.
There is a cathedral of autumn leaves
as I stroll down the lane,
There is a rose window in every puddle
whole and unshattered.

What grows behind stone walls?
Not me. No, not me.

– Stephanie Noble

Namaste

(May my higher Self meet your higher Self)

My heart speaks
to your heart
and your heart
speaks to mine
and our eyes
and our tongues
and our skin
do not get
in between
But you know
that I know
and I know
that you know
that Somewhere
Forever
the Beloved
takes us In.

Blessed Be

– Lois Ames

Sinai

Because you brought me out of Egypt
you expect me to serve you forever
and let bygones be bygones. I object
to the deal Moses made. Having been there
when you spoke, I remember how Moses
said you were OK. And I remember
the idols I used to invoke, losses
like that demand some kind of payback. Where
were you, Omnipotent One, when people
cried out to you on the stake? Does the char
of human flesh excite your sense of smell?
Or do you lean more toward the odor
of a death camp? God, will you punish me
for asking what you've done for me lately?

– Joanne Seltzer

Consequences

A set of maroon-covered volumes embossed in gold stood behind glass in the living room. I remember only one page: colored in poisonous greens and oranges, outlined in a thick black border, was an illustration of the gates of Hell. A devil with a pitchfork prodded writhing, screaming bodies into the fire-breathing mouth of a huge dragon. The fire, the naked limbs, and the contorted heads dangling from the dragon's mouth terrified me. I alternated between avoiding the picture and obsessively seeking it out, looking just long enough to assure myself that it was every bit as sickening and unbearable as I remembered, then snapping the book shut and vowing never to look again. I was too young to read the words, and afraid to ask their meaning. But I knew: this was the punishment for Sin. I wasn't sure what one had to do to deserve it, but whatever it was, this was what could come for you.

> *"I was too young to read the words, and afraid to ask their meaning. But I knew: this was the punishment for Sin."*

Upstairs, the Son of God watched over me. A cardboard bas-relief of the Madonna and child hung next to my bed. This pair—the calm, adoring mother and her fat contented baby—stared at me as I thrashed around in the boredom of summer-afternoon naps. I would kick the picture, cover the baby's face with my foot, and hate him for wallowing in his mother's arms. My own mother's lap was full, with the toddler who had usurped me clinging to her, and the new baby growing inside.

One afternoon, when I grew tired of chewing the large wad of gum I had smuggled upstairs, I looked for a place to save it. I pressed it against the picture. It stuck hard. When I pulled the gum away Mary's face came with it. I pressed again. The face of the baby Jesus peeled off even more easily than His mother's. I worked diligently. Soon there was nothing left but rough gray cardboard. I could now get out my crayons and draw in a scene much more to my liking. Whatever short-term

consequences I might suffer for this defiling would be worth
the relief of removing that fat complacent baby from his mother's
lap forever. As for the long-term consequences, I could now
think of one good reason why, if I should die before I awake,
I would surely be shoveled into the dragon's burning mouth.

– Elizabeth Stoessl

Prayer

O God, I am a mere speck in your grand creation
    my doings just a tiny whisper on boisterous planet Earth

O God, I am the center of my universe,
    my daily doings are terribly important to me
    (and I hope to you)

O God of Infinite Wisdom,
    Show me a place to nestle between my seeming insignificance
    and my overwhelming importance.

– Pam Thielman

Meditation

There is an Invisible Screen
and when I go through It
I am a different I

– Lois Ames

A Prayer

This paltry song
is like the small vowels
of a child
learning to speak

But it may be
one clear sweet note
in the long symphony
poets play for God

– Lois Ames

The Living Water

I once spoke so clearly.
My words tumbling freely like a waterfall.
I filled small ponds beneath me
with thoughts,
stirring pools that yearned for my current.

Now I fumble for words of meaning.
I have sensed the shallowness of my own pond.
I thirst for stronger downpour
from a new Source —
The Living Water.

And I, seemingly strong fountain,
feel like a trickle next to Your cascade.
As I come for communion,
to Your crystal clear lake,
reflecting my Soul.

– Caryn Summers

Channel

Exploding before my startled eyes
a glimmering gateway,
dimensional light
so pure
it hurts...
sparkles sounding
no time or space,
love energy
radiating
energy
I cannot grasp
energy
I cannot contain
in my modest form
of flesh.

Only seconds
through this portal of spinning gold
where souls have searched and sung,
my mind stirs
heart flows
eyes melt
and I remember...
as though awakened
from the most sluggish sleep
what it once was like
when in a different life
I stepped through
to the other side of the door.

– Nina Silver

Inclination

Living trees
    bend before
Your unseen breath,
    Lord.
Supple, strong
    in flexiblity
They bow themselves
    with grace.

Unseen Spirit,
Am I so inclined?

– Nancy Spiegelberg

They are aligned with the universe —

Who listen for the harmonies, not just the tunes
  and are moved by the rhythms
Who watch for the patterns, not only the colors
  and are comforted by the dark
Who relish the shade, as well as the sun
  and are soothed by the rain
Who promote peace, not confrontation
  and are sustained by balance
Who believe in all the gods, not just one
  and are caught up in unity

— Jean Carpenter

The Stumbling Warrior

I am a stumbling warrior:
    I rush outside
Seeking the fullness of the moon
    I do not want to miss
        the Asking Time.

I crash into the vacuum cleaner:
    Stub my toe in the dark
    Throw on the light
    Spill my water
    Drench my sage and tobacco
    Wet my feather.

Coyote is close at hand
Trickster that he is
    Makes me laugh
Before I can let out
    a curse of anger
    "Got me!" I laugh
    at Invisible Coyote.

Finally, out the back door
    I crash into a spider's web
    wed to the clematis vine
    and the screen door.
    Oh! I am shocked
        at my carelessness.

But Spider is patient
She will weave again.
    I sullenly move into
        the clearing by the pear tree

I stoop to light my sage;
All is ready now.
The White Light eye of the moon
    winks to me,
    I raise myself
    in a precision movement
    that makes a thunking
    connection between
    the loaded pear branch above me
        and my head.

The moon laughs,
Coyote howls
The struggling embers in the sage bowl
    fizzle and die.
My tobacco pouch, holding
    Sacred offering
    is damp from the spilt water.

What shall I ask for?

Grandmother Moon,
    Help my wobbly warrior legs
    move with grace.
And, Grandmother Moon—
    Maybe I need to readjust my boundaries?

                – Mary Diane Hausman

Prayer

God of Time and Space
Be with me in this sacred moment,
The only time I have,
Help me to stay in this
    one-now-only moment,
Not in the moments that stretch
    back to my birth—delighting and confusing me,
Nor in the moments that loom far into my future,
    tempting me with their newness and
    frightening me with their uncertainty,
Help me to stay in this one-now-only moment
    that you have created.

– Pam Thielman

What Unfolds Before Me

the incense sends
curling streams into the room
it is smoke speaking smoke
a language I am willing to learn

coyote has his new home
and the promised food
he will eat and tell me stories
I wait for revelations
from the full moon
and the no-moon sky

I wait for the hawk
to land on my snow covered path
The hawk will speak hawk
and leave a tail feather on the trail

I travel to a high white place
smooth as glazed porcelain
there is no language here
but a cloud of calm
I am willing to learn

– Connie Hershey

That Deepest Meditation

There is a prison to which I willingly go
without peace, without release,
its' single-pointed madness that I know,
and only you can find me there
beneath the folds on folds.
This is not separate from
it is the deepest form of meditation,
where pleasure extends as far into time
as we have time,
where the woman of shame
meets the girl of pain,
and you embrace us, join us, heal us
of the wound that has no name.
This is home, the place where we vow
a life together of passages, healings.
So race we to the razor's edge now
to taste such unbearable lightness of being.

– Susan Galbraith

Prayer

We accept these gifts of the earth with gratitude and humility;
May we always cultivate and use the land's bounty wisely and
    frugally.

We acknowledge with wonder the beauty and power of the
    universe;
May we deal with all its creatures in a spirit of tolerance,
    respect, and good will.

We come together today with family and friends in joy and love;
May we ever find, and give, comfort and sustenance in our
    relationships.

We join our hearts and hands to pray for balance, harmony,
    and peace;
May our prayers be linked with the spiritual energy of the
    universe.

–Jean Carpenter

If Only I Had Known You

Lord,
    I crawled
    across the barrenness
        to You
        with my empty cup
    uncertain
        in asking
            any small drop
            of refreshment.

If only
    I had known You
    better
I'd have come
Running
With a bucket.

– Nancy Spiegelberg

Cursing the Prayers

my prayers are not creative
or rhythmic incantations
but stumbled mutterings
over wallet photos of my children
spilled drops of English tea
I listen
for a busboy's knock
at the door

my prayers lack form
and I burn broken bits
of incense in an ashtray
to clear the stinking hotel room
not one stick whole
nothing integrated
I drift
from consciousness
toward the foreign city of sleep

these prayers are near death
but without the comforting final chords
whatever hears these prayers
will not be flattered
or amused
this is poverty
more hungry
than an empty bowl of rice

my prayers are scraps
shall I scrounge
for the right red thread
to piece them into stars
or wait
for a package to arrive
from India or New Mexico
whole cloth in which to wrap myself

– Connie Hershey

Pagan

for Muriel Rukeyser

At home
in the countryside
I make the decision
to leave your book
—overdue at the library—
face up, "promiscuous"
out in the sun.

Pagan.

I laugh to see
this was our religion
all along.

Hidden
even from ourselves
taught
early
not to touch
the earth.

Years of white gloves
straight seamed hose.
"Being good girls."
Scripture like chains.
Dogma like flies.
Smiles like locks
and lies.

—Alice Walker

Simple Request

God, I don't beleive
You promised
    instant deliverance from
    every inconvenience by
    simply dictating
        our wishes
        one by one
to You.
A tremor disquiets my spirit
    and I wonder
    when I read in Psalms:
        "He gave them
        their request;
        but sent
        leanness
        into their soul."
If anytime
    Your desires and mine
    happen not to coincide—
Give me Your will, God!
And fatness for my soul.

— *Nancy Spiegelberg*

A Prayer

O Creator, source of all life
Shine your light in my heart.
And through my hands
Manifest your love.
Calm my doubts and
Unlock any gates on the path
You have set me.
Let my eyes see the beauty
My ears hear the harmony
My skin feel the texture
My tongue taste the bounty
And my nose smell the sweetness
of your earthly garden,
Knowing that through my senses
you experience the joy
of your own creation.
Let my words and actions
stem from love, not fear.
Let me be ever aware of
my connection with all that is.
Gently prod me from the traps
of wallowing in the past
or living too much for the future.
Let me savor the moment
Knowing that it is always
your greatest gift.
For this and all your creation
I am truly thankful. Amen

– Stephanie Noble

Yes

you know it is late and my arms feel heavy
as I try to move
lifting my chest to make room for the next breath
I find it is heavy too
the dark window panes reflect
the right angles contained here in this room
one thing about this meditation class is
that I find out how a week disappears magically
without time to meditate
I do acknowledge my own awareness
as I drive down these rural roads to deliver
my children to school, myself to appointments
a furrowed field trenched with snow and brought to life
with a flock of geese pecking and nibbling,
stretching their long necks, resting until the next signal
to stand straight and still before they
telepathically plan their flight
each bird visualizing lifting into its precise place
variations in snow and ice across wetlands
what formations the lines of spruce point to above themselves
the afternoon hour that I hold myself hungrily
when the fields of tall grasses go orange and
whole forests are filled with violet trunks
and I want to stop driving and step out of my car
and feel my feet touching the earth and I want
to be absorbed into the light and the growing lives
of these trees and grasses

– Connie Hershey

Take Me Down, Grandmama God

Take me down, Grandmama God.
Take me down under.
Take me down Grandmama God,
    under my fear of aloneness.
Take me down, Grandmama God,
    under money and mortgages and mortality.
Take me down, Grandmama God,
    under my body's ache for a loving partner.
Take me down, Grandmama God,
    under my soul's ache for order and beauty.
Take me down, Grandmama God,
    under all my judgments of myself.
Take me down, Grandmama God,
    under my bone weariness tonight.
Take me down, Grandmama God,
    into the Earth, Your womb, Your cradle.
Take me down, Grandmama God,
    into your warm arms.
Hold me, Grandmama God, hold me.

– Mary Feagan

"Put Down Your Pen," Says Grandmama God

"Put down your pen," Says Grandmama God
"Breathe.
Relax.
Feel the sun
on your face.
Stop the race
To get things done.
Everything is in place
Everything is OK.
For twenty minutes it can stay just so
While you play,
While you pray, while you stay with Me."

– Mary Feagan

I'd Rather Run

I'd rather run
    across hot coals
Than sit here, Lord.

Running seems
    so much more
    commendable.
But if You're
    telling me to stay,
I'll learn somehow
    to sit with vigor.

– Nancy Spiegelberg

Meditation: Traveling by Car to Dharamsala, India

riding the reckless rim
tightly coiled breath buds
give way to small breaths
which pulse into large and deep
inhalations, invocations

it becomes necessary to open
all the doors of the mind's hotel
look out on this blooming wildernesss
the Himalayas pass through these doors
as easily as a sleeping monkey or a sunlit goat

it is necessary to lean outward on the curves
no resisitance, ready to be unfooted in that wide space
to hold both hands to your chest, remembering your own
radiance
to release your self into the moment when you will fall free

– Connie Hershey

Repeat Performance

O God of Second Chances
and New Beginnings

Here I am again.

– *Nancy Spiegelberg*

I Sit Still Better Now

I sit still better now.
This morning I did it for a whole half-hour.
I just held my doll and breathed.
It takes the opposite of power...
It takes collapsing, yielding, relaxing
My hold on my soul.
Maybe for me, right now it's most
Like hovering, as a hummingbird
Furiously beats its weightless wings
To stay still while it drinks the nectar from a flower
Or drinks the sweet water from my neighbor grandma's dish.
But She feeds me delicious food anyway,
However my soul comes to Her table.

– Mary Feagan

Meditation on the Lord's Prayer

Our Father, source of liberating love, author of goodness and kindness, our constant strength and providence. We who call you "father" are brothers and sisters; each one loved without reserve, each one expecting the full, rich inheritance that you have promised.

You wait for us in heaven, our homeland, our final destination. At the end of our pilgrimage, when we finally see you face to face, when we know the full measure of your embrace, then will we know the fulfillment of our deepest and most mysterious yearnings and the profound peace that comes from being home. It is then that all peoples will...

Call your name hallowed. Then will all mysteries be revealed. Then will all men and women praise you for your wisdom and mercy and sing the glory of your works.

Your kingdom shall have come, your will shall be accomplished. Your children shall live in peace, harmony, love, and justice under your protective mantle. Like tiles in a mosaic, each will take their place in your grand design. The hopes and dreams that had been buried so deeply in our hearts that they never before had found expression will be realized. For this journey, Father, we need nourishment, so we ask you to...

Give us the bread we need each day. For our sustenance and in renewal of your promises, your Word is made flesh and blood anew. May this food give our spirits the courage and perseverance that is needed for a life of loving service. Keep us always mindful that you await our arrival eagerly and that you have already prepared a perfect banquet in our honor.

Forgive us our wrongs, as we have forgiven those who have wronged us. Your son has relieved us of the burden of our sins; we ask for the mercy to forgive ourselves so that we may truly be liberated from guilt, remorse, and fear. Likewise, Father, help us to replace our judgments, criticisms, and grudges with acceptance, compassion, and understanding of our fellow pilgrims. And finally, when we near the end of our journey...

Do not put us to the test, but save us from the evil one. Give us the strength to be ever faithful to the demands of the Christian Life. Keep us steadfast in hope so that at the darkest moment, just before we know the dawn of your glory, we may resist the most insidious of temptations, despair.

May your love and justice abide forever in the heavenly community.

– Sheila Gorg

The Breathing, The Endless News

Every god is lonely, an exile
composed of parts: elk horn,
cloven hoof. Receptacle

for wishes, each god is empty
without us, penitent,
raking our yards into windblown piles....

Children know this: they are
the trailings of gods. Their eyes
hold nothing at birth then fill slowly

with the myth of ourselves. Not so the dolls,
out for the count, each toe pouting from
the slumped-over toddler clothes:

no blossoming there. So we
give our children dolls, and
they know just what to do—

line them up and shoot them.
With every execution
doll and god grow stronger.

– Rita Dove

Meditation

I shed selves
like snakeskins
trying to forget
self, trying to melt
into the Self

– Lois Ames

Fanfare

Quietly
He called me.
Humbly speaking
it was no extravaganza;
earth scarcely noticed.
Yet I've been told
that beyond galaxies
a fanfare broke out
when I said "Yes" to Him
and took His Name.

– Nancy Spiegelberg

Psalm

we are mountains
surrounded by an abyss.

oceans
where tiny things are swallowed
by bigger ones,

the sky
trampled by sun, moon, stars,
planets, clouds

temples of ivory
abandoned with incense

groundhogs
whose shadows are real

–Joanne Seltzer

Meditation

Meditation is not about the should's and shouldn'ts
is not about the would's and couldn'ts
nor about the will do's, did them, and have dones.
Meditation is
in the being in...exactly where you are
    right now.
What is it you are hearing? Listen.
What are you seeing in your mind's eye?
    Follow, but keep your distance.
What is your breath doing?
Think, breathe in, breathe out.
    Breathe in. Breathe out.
Leave the rest at the door.

– Susan Galbraith

Kwanyin at Christmas

(Come kiss the manger where he lies
That is your bliss above the skies—Robert Southwell)

Coming near the bed
With eyes popping like two lightning bugs
The Hag gasps—puckers up her mug
To kiss a child's head.

She waltzes through the dusty room
—Zooms from one emptiness into another;
Time transforms
Into a breath of fog and scent of pine.

The Old Bag chants incantations.
Stars fill with affections,
Moons fume away,
The earth slowly sways with four seasons.

With a lotus in her teeth, she bleats:
"O God, what has thrown my mind astray?"

Devils and monsters shiver
Jitter and jump into the endless Hole,
And as they fall they howl:
"How unfair! It's totally illogical for God to become a dumb man."

–Joyce Cook

Dialectical Romance

He asked if she believed in God
so she looked him in the eye
before answering No but he wouldn't
give in: Not even a little bit?
Then because it was raining and
they were walking down a path others
might have called paradise, she added
Not even a little—though at times
she wished she could. It was a lie
but she was being polite; besides,
they had just turned from Suicide Point
and it seemed the social thing to say.

He believed there was a force but didn't feel
compelled to give it a name; it needn't be
embodied. She thought of the Virgin
at Bergamo, marble limbs dressed in dusty
crinolines, a life-sized Barbie doll.

Some force has to have made all this—
his armsweep sending more droplets down,
gravel protesting like gritting teeth—
and then set everything loose in it.

So God's given up? she ventured, which made him
swallow. Remembering where they'd been, then,
those soaked crags and lake-stunned altitudes,
she dredged up for his sake a comparison
from computers: a program so large
there could be no answer
except in working it through.

– Rita Dove

Ribbon of Hours

Time travels through me like a river
flowing so fast I sometimes get caught in the rapids.
I want to slow the forced journey or turn around—go back—
but the current pushes me on.
Clinging to branches along the way
I try to fight against the flight of time, hold on to a precious
    moment
to taste it, touch it, make it a part of me,
but I must open my grasp and watch it float away behind me.

On through this ribbon of hours I speed
past family, past friends, past moments, past loves, past myself.
Far behind I leave a small girl
whose imagination took her everywhere but here.
Nearer—but too far away—a young woman remains, learning,
listening, loving, grasping for life's mysteries,
not knowing each bit of time could disappear like a grain of
    sand.
Time moved through me then like honey—slow and sweet.

Reflections still linger, though the images are gone,
of births, unions, separations, sorrows, and ecstasies.
I race ahead and I must cut the cords, let it all go.
I do not wish it.
It is harder than I ever imagined,
but the flowing continues
and I am always farther ahead than where I am
on this river that flows through me.
I cannot hold it and I cannot change its course, but I can flow
    with it.

– *Cynthia C. Rosso*

The Contributors

Lois Ames holds a degree from Smith College and a Master's in Psychiatric Social Work from the University of Chicago. Her parallel lives as a clinical social worker, writer and spiritual seeker have taken her to China, India, Russia and Mexico. She is the author of several articles and books, including *Anne Sexton: A Self-Portrait in Letters* (Houghton-Mifflin, 1995). Lois, the mother of two grown children, lives, writes and is healing from breast cancer in Sudbury, Massachusetts.

Susan D. Anderson holds a Master's Degree in Early Childhood Development and a Doctorate in Instructional Leadership. She is currently writing a non-fiction book on psychological abuse in the family. She lived on an island in Casco Bay for two years while ghost writing a self-help book about marriage and collecting observations for a book about the relationship between the natural environment and the writing life. She currently resides in Amherst, Mass.

Lynn Andrews lives in Los Angeles, where she devotes herself to writing, counseling, teaching, and living the Medicine Way. She is the author of several best-selling books including *Jaguar Woman, Star Woman, Crystal Woman, Walk in Spirit, Prayers for the Seasons of Life,* and newly released *Love & Power.*

Maya Angelou is the author of five books of poetry and *On the Pulse of Morning,* the 1992 Presidential Inaugural poem. She has also written several best-selling books, including *I Know Why the Caged Bird sings, Gather Together in My Name,* and *Heart of a Woman.* She is a Reynolds Professor at Wake Forest University, Winston-Salem, North Carolina.

Kathryn Elizabeth Antea lives, works and writes in Golden, Colorado.

Z. (Zsuzsanna) Budapest is one the founding mothers of today's women's spirituality movement. *The Holy Book of Women's Mysteries,* was one of the first women's spirituality books available in the U.S. or Europe. She has gone on to be a prolific writer. Her latest two works include *Goddess in the Office,* and *Goddess in the Bedroom.*

Ann M. Ridley Butterfield is a nine-year breast cancer survivor. She holds a B.A. in English from Northwestern University and has been employed for 18 years at a national education association. She was a member of the Writers' Roundtable at Iowa State University and has published fiction in the student magazine, *Sketch.* She currently resides in Vienna, VA.

Su Byron lives in Sarasota, Florida where she co-edits the Sarasota Arts Review. Her poetry collections include *Paris Poems* (1984-86); *Lament of No One Special* (1988); *The Jack Poems* (1989); *Biography: 10 Prose Poems* (1990); *Spilling Beer* (1991); and, *Flagging Down the Angels* (1993).

Jean Carpenter has raised a family of three while pursuing an on-and-off career in publishing and following her Air Force husband from one assignment to the next. Creative writing is a new activity—and a new thrill—that fills old needs. She lives and writes in Fairfax, VA.

Leah B. Cates believes that physical, emotional, and spiritual experiences are intertwined. Thus, her own lifelong experience with a rare congenital heart disease influences her artistic expression. Leah has previously written for journalistic and technical publications. This is her first published creative writing. Leah lives in Falls Church, VA.

Dawn Chamberlain works by day as a social worker helping homeless persons find housing and services in Washington, D.C., and as a counselor with at-risk children in Maryland. At night, she writes. Her other loves include mythology and world folklore, women's studies and music—particularly Brazilian jazz.

Neva A. Clayton is a freelance writer pursuing her role as a healer through therapeutic massage and counseling. She enjoys a lifelong love of nature, and lives with four cats in the town of Bridgewater in the Shenandoah Valley of Virginia. She shares her back yard and herb garden with birds, possums, squirrels, and skunks.

Joyce Cook is a socio-linguist and poet. She has taught at the University of Tel Aviv, San Diego City College, and most recently was the Graduate/Undergraduate Advisor in the English Department at Stanford University. She has spent most of her professional life as an educator/administrator and is currently located in Bridgeport, CT.

Virginia Butchart Cowie is a 50 year-old woman who has just begun to bloom. Her life is taking a new, exciting path that is propelled by her spirituality. She successfully raised two daughters who were her life. They grew up and were on their

own when Virginia began to discover herself. She has written
an article on her spirituality that is scheduled to be published
by *Encore* magazine. Virginia pursues her new passion in
Waterford, MI.

Rita Dove was the Poet Laureate of the United States from
1993-94. She is the author of *Thomas and Beulah,* a Pulitzer
Prize winning poetry collection. She has written several other
books of poetry including *The Yellow House on the Corner,* and
a novel entitled, *Through the Ivory Gate.* She is a professor at
the University of Virginia.

Mary Feagan is an artist, art teacher, and poet. A nun for
eleven years and then twice married, she is finally paying
attention to her dear self, to her intuitions, inspirations,
whims, and pleasures. Mary lives and writes in Duluth, GA.

CB Follett has had poems published in many poetry publications, including *Calyx, Green Fuse, South Coast Poetry Bone.*
She has also had poems published in several anthologies and
eight of her poems have been awarded prizes. One of her
poems was nominated for Pushcart, 1993. She has published a
book of her work entitled, *The Latitudes of Their Going* (1993).
She currently lives in Sausalito, CA.

a.c. fowler (Anne Carroll) is an Episcopal priest and rector of
St. John's Church in Jamaica Plain, MA. Her poems have
appeared in many journals and little magazines. She lives in
Jamaica Plain with her husband and children.

Susan Galbraith graduated from Tufts University *summa cum
laude* and *Phi Beta Kappa* with degrees in English and Drama.
Born and raised in Indonesia, she continues to search for the
equivalent of the Balinese Village in her work and community,

where the arts and spirituality are honored and woven into the fabric of every day life. For the past few years, she has been involved in quite a balancing act: writing and directing opera and theatre; teaching and running her own yoga studio, *The Creative Body;* and raising her son, Eamonn in Reston, Virginia. Poetry has always been kept a private activity, listening to that very quiet voice of the soul and marking touchstone moments of the inner life.

Sheila Gorg lives, works, grieves and grows in Northern Virginia. Her volunteer interests include writing for and editing church publications and promoting social justice.

Salome Harasty has published essays and articles in local and regional church publications in St. Petersburg, Florida. She holds a degree in Theology and has fifteen years of experience in professional church ministry. *Labor Day* is one of her first attempts at writing short stories. She takes the high-profile issue of homosexuality and combines it with the ancient value and dedication of a mother's love.

Mary Diane Hausman was born and raised in the Texas Hill country. She now lives in Little Ferry, New Jersey where she writes, paints, and analyzes computer software. Her works have appeared in *Women and Recovery, Relevant Times, At the Crossroads,* and *Wide Open Magazine.* Her story, "The Feeding" won first place in the Pennwriters, 'In Other Words' contest. She teaches healing and self-empowerment workshops using writing and storytelling and is currently working on a novel about growing up in Texas.

Connie Hershey is the founder of Artifact Press, Ltd., in Concord, Massachusetts, which has published one book to date: *Truth and Lies That Press for Life: 60 Los Angeles Poets.*

Her own poems will be published in *Shooting Star Review, On the Bus,* and *Atom Mind.*

Rochelle Lynn Holt is the author of numerous poetry volumes, short stories, novellas, and the recent, *Panes—Fiction as Therapy* (Columbia Pacific Univ. Press, San Rafael, CA, 1993). She has held 57 jobs since the age of 14 and has lived in five states, most recently in Ft. Meyers, Florida.

D.E. Irons lives and works in York, Pennsylvania. She holds a B.A. in Journalism and Communications from Point Park College, Pittsburgh, PA. Her poetry has been published in several college literary magazines and most recently by Sparrowgrass Press.

Gina Jones is a mother of two and a sixth grade teacher of language arts in Green Bay, WI. She has co-authored three books, *Earth Dance Drum, Listen to the Drum,* and *The Healing Drum* with her husband, Blackwolf Jones. Gina is currently collaborating with two Wisconsin Ojibwa medicine women on the celebration of womanhood and seeks to honor her world through poetry, fiction and personal reflection.

Laura H. Kennedy holds a B.A. in English and a M.A. in Counseling. She has been widely published in *Beanfeast, High Tide, Kumquat Meringue,* and *ELF: Eclectic Literary Forum.* She has placed in several poetry competitions and has done a number of readings of her own work. She now lives in Stratford, CT.

Lisa Miles resides in Pittsburgh, Pennsylvania. She is a professional violinist who works collaboratively with artists of various disciplines. She has been a member of a women's cross-disciplinary creative group for a number of years. She is currently working on a biography of a woman artist originally from Pittsburgh who moved to Greenwich Village in the 1930's.

Stephanie Noble is the author of *Tapping the Wisdom Within, A Guide to Joyous Living,* a non-fiction spiritually oriented book that fosters self-acceptance and a deep sense of belonging, published by Inside Out Books. She lives in Marin County, California with her artist husband.

Jacqueline Marni Olkin lives in her home town of Reston, Virginia, where she works as an editor and graphic designer. She enjoys hiking, writing, working out, movies and museums, a good cup of tea, general silliness, and the company of her loved ones and friends.

Carol C. Ordal has worked as a chemist, teacher, homemaker, social worker, and editor. She currently edits a company's web site while exploring the world of computers and the global internet. However, for exploring her inner world, working with words, and reading for inspiration, she prefers the simple comfort of a pencil, a piece of paper, a real book, and a quiet desk or coffee shop. Then the letters, journal entries, poems, bookmarks, postcards, and stationary she loves to create can be born. She writes and creates in Urbana, IL.

Cynthia C. Rosso hung up her dancing shoes about 10 years ago for lack of lumbar support and found creative solace in her other love—writing. She earns her living in Sterling, Virginia as a publishing manager for a large educational association and enjoys the new challenges she faces each day. Among her greatest accomplishments are a son and a daughter who, now grown, are going on to make their own accomplishments.

Joanne Seltzer's poems have appeared widely in anthologies such as *When I Am an Old Woman I Shall Wear Purple,* and in literary journals such as *The Croton Review* and *Kalliope.* She has also published short fiction, literary essays, translations of French poetry and three poetry chapbooks of her own work. She lives and writes in Schenectady, New York.

Nina Silver is a body/mind psychotherapist, musician and artist whose writings on feminism, sexuality, political theory, and metaphysics have appeared in numerous publications. She is currently a Doctoral candidate in Psychology at the Union Institute, where she is working on a book that integrates feminism, depth psychology, and the body/mind principles of Wilhelm Reich. Her volume of poetry, *Birthing,* will be published soon by Woman in the Moon Publications. She pursues her work and writing in Worthington, MA.

Nancy Spiegelberg had her first poem published when she was 9 years old in the *Amherst News Times.* In 1995, she published her second book of poetry, *I'd Like to Ask God* (Harvest House). Nancy was a registered nurse for many years and most recently worked for Youth With A Mission, an organization that does Bible distribution, evangelism and charitable work in the US and in impoverished countries. Mother of 3 grown children, she currently lives in Pennsylvania with her daughter, son-in-law and 3 grandchildren who love to play with the "little kid dressed up in Grandma clothes."

Elizabeth Stoessl is a writer and former librarian who lives in Springfield, Virginia.

Elizabeth Anne Stolfi is an educator and psychotherapist. She began her spiritual journey in 1993. Part of that journey has included the healing power of writing and poetry. She lives and works in New Jersey.

Pam Stolpman is a poet and short story writer. She lives in Alexandria, Virginia.

Caryn Summers is a nurse, accomplished author, public speaker and publisher. Her writing is an extension of her professional and spiritual pursuits. She is the author of several books, including *Circle of Health: Recovery Through the Medicine Wheel, Caregiver, Caretaker, Inspirations for Caregivers* and *the Girl, the Rock and the Water.* The mother of 2 grown children and 2 lively grandchildren, Caryn lives, works, writes and plays in Salt Lake City, Utah.

Marie A. Sylvester began keeping a journal at age 8 and continues keeping that journal faithfully to this day. She has an Associate Degree in Communications and is working towards the completion of her B.A. in Journalism. By day, she works as an executive secretary; by night, she works on her writing projects, including a fiction novel that takes place in Atlantic City at the turn of the century. She currently resides in Interlaken, New Jersey.

Pam Thielman lives and writes in Arlington, Virginia.

Alice Walker is the author of *The Color Purple,* which won an American Book Award, a Pulitzer Prize, and was an acclaimed motion picture. Her latest book, *The Temple of My Familiar,* was on the *New York Times* Best-Seller list for four months.

About the Editor/Compiler

Mollie Cox Bryan lives with her husband Eric and cats Isis and Troubles (who are both aptly named) in Reston, VA. She holds a B.A. in Journalism and Communications from Point Park College, Pittsburgh, PA. She has studied poetry with Geraldine Connolly at the Writer's Center, Bethesda, MD, and with Cornelius Eady as part of the George Washington University's Jenny McKean Moore Poetry Workshop. Her poetry has been published in college literary magazines and most recently in *The Beltane Papers* and *Deus Loci,* in which she is featured as an Honorable Mention in their White Mice Poetry contest. She is currently working on her first collection of poetry.

She grew up in Raccoon Township, a small rural area just outside Pittsburgh, PA, writing poems, plays and stories. After going to college, marrying and subsequently divorcing, she found her way back to poetry and its cathartic healing quality that has helped her find her way to Herself and to Spirit.

About the Photographer

For more than 20 years, **Shannon Caudill** has expressed his honor for women by respectfully capturing their spirit and form in his photographs. His images of women of all ages, sizes, and color artistically express powerful moments of feminine celebration, ritual and prayer.

Shannon's photographic images are unique in their simplicity and elegance. He works with the principle of the feminine archetype, reflecting moods and emotions through form rather than facial expressions. Using only natural light in his photographs, Shannon enjoys shooting in a variety of environments, from man-made linear structures to the purest elements in nature.

Born in Virginia, Shannon has lived across the United States and Europe. He now resides in Salt Lake City, Utah where desert meets mountain and provides a dramatic backdrop for his models and photography.

Suggested Readings

Anderson, Lorraine (Ed.) *Sisters of the Earth*. New York: Random House, 1991.

Andrews, Lynn. *Medicine Woman*. San Francisco: Harper & Row, 1983.

Andrews, Lynn. *Jaguar Woman*. San Francisco: Harper & Row, 1986.

Andrews, Lynn. *Star Woman*. New York: Warner Books, 1986.

Andrews, Lynn. *Crystal Woman*. New York: Warner Books, 1987.

Andrews, Lynn. *Walk in Spirit, Prayers for the Seasons of Life*. Acacia, 1996.

Andrews, Lynn. *Love & Power*. New York: Harper Collins, 1997.

Angelou, Maya. *I Know Why the Caged-Bird Sings*. New York: Bantam Doubleday Dell, 1971.

Angelou, Maya. *Oh, Pray My Wings Are Gonna Fit Me Well*. New York: Random House, 1975.

Budapest, Z. *The Holy Book of Women's Mysteries*. Wingbow Press, 1989.

Christ, Carol C. & Plaskow, Judith, (Eds). *WomanSpirit Rising: A Feminist Reader in Religion*. New York: Harper Collins, 1992.

Dove, Rita. *Grace Notes*. New York: W.W. Norton, 1989.

Fox, John. *Finding What You Didn't Lose: Expressing Your Truth and Creativity Through Poem-Making*. New York: G.P. Putnam & Sons, 1995.

Leonard, Linda Schierse. *The Wounded Woman*. Boulder, CO: Shambhala Publications, 1982.

Leonard, Linda Schierse. *Witness to the Fire: Creativity & The Veil of Addiction*. Boston, MA: Shambhala Publications, 1989.

Lindbergh, Anne Morrow. *Gift From the Sea*. New York: Random House, 1991.

Olsen, Tillie. *Silences*. New York: Dell Publishing, 1978.

Starhawk. *The Spiral Dance: A Rebirth of the Ancient Religion of the Great Goddess*. New York: Harper & Row, 1989.

Walker, Alice. *The Color Purple*. New York: Harcourt, Brace & Co, 1982.

Walker, Alice. *The Temple of My Familiar*. New York: Harcourt, Brace & Co., 1989.

Walker, Alice. *Her Blue Body Everything We Know: Earthling Poems*. San Diego: Harcourt, Brace & Co., 1991.

Walker, Barbara. *Woman's Dictionary of Symbols and Sacred Objects*. San Francisco: Harper & Row, 1988.

Index

Commune-a-Key Publishing and Seminars

Commune-a-Key Publishing and Seminars was established in 1992. Our mission statement, "Communicating Keys to Growth and Empowerment," describes our effort to publish books that inspire and promote personal growth and wellness. Our books and products provide powerful ways to care for, discover and heal ourselves and others.

Our audience includes health care professionals and counselors, caregivers, women, men, people interested in Native American traditions—anyone interested in personal growth, psychology and inspiration. We hope you enjoy this book! If you have any comments, questions, or would like to be on our mailing list for future products and seminars, please write or call us at the address and phone number below.

Commune-a-Key Publishing
P.O. Box 58637
Salt Lake City, UT 84158
•
1-800-983-0600

ORDERING INFORMATION

Commune-a-Key Publishing has a variety of books and products. For further information on our books, or if you would like to receive a catalog, please write or call us at the address and phone number listed below.

Our authors are also available for seminars, workshops and lectures. Please call our toll-free number for further information.

Commune-a-Key Publishing
P.O. Box 58637
Salt Lake City, UT 84158
•
1-800-983-0600